SHUT YOUR MONKEY

SHUT YOUR MONKEY

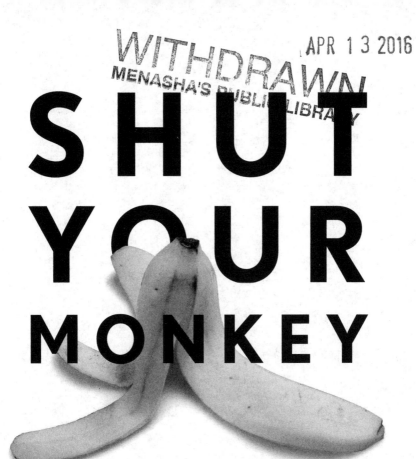

How to Control Your Inner Critic and Get More Done

by Danny Gregory

HOW
BOOKS
Cincinnati, Ohio
www.howdesign.com

For more excellent books and resources for designers, visit *www.howdesign.com*.

19 18 17 16 15   5 4 3 2 1

ISBN-10: 1-4403-4113-3

ISBN-13: 978-1-4403-4113-7

eISBN-10: 1-4403-4117-6

eISBN-13: 978-1-4403-4117-5

Distributed in Canada by Fraser Direct

100 Armstrong Avenue

Georgetown, Ontario, Canada L7G 5S4

Tel: (905) 877-4411

Distributed in the U.K. and Europe by F&W Media International, LTD

Pynes Hill Court, Pynes Hill, Rydon Lane, Exeter, EX2 5 SP, U.K.

Tel: (+44) 1392 797680, Fax: (+44) 1626 323319

E-mail: *enquiries@fwmedia.com*

Distributed in Australia by Capricorn Link

P.O. Box 704, Windsor, NSW 2756 Australia

Tel: (02) 4560-1600

Images © Smithsonian Institute, Wikimedia Commons, Cardcow.com, Los Angeles Public Library, iStockphoto.com/GlobalP/Gizelka/SergeyTimofeev/Barbs_eye_view/perception_photography/Brendan Hunter/RobertLevy, and 123RF/Paco Ayala/zimmytws/stillfx/Sorapop Udomsri.

Illustrations by Danny Gregory

Cover and interior design by Rachel Willey

Edited by Amy Owen

Production coordinated by Greg Nock

a content + ecommerce company

For you—and all the great creative things you are going to do.

CONTENTS

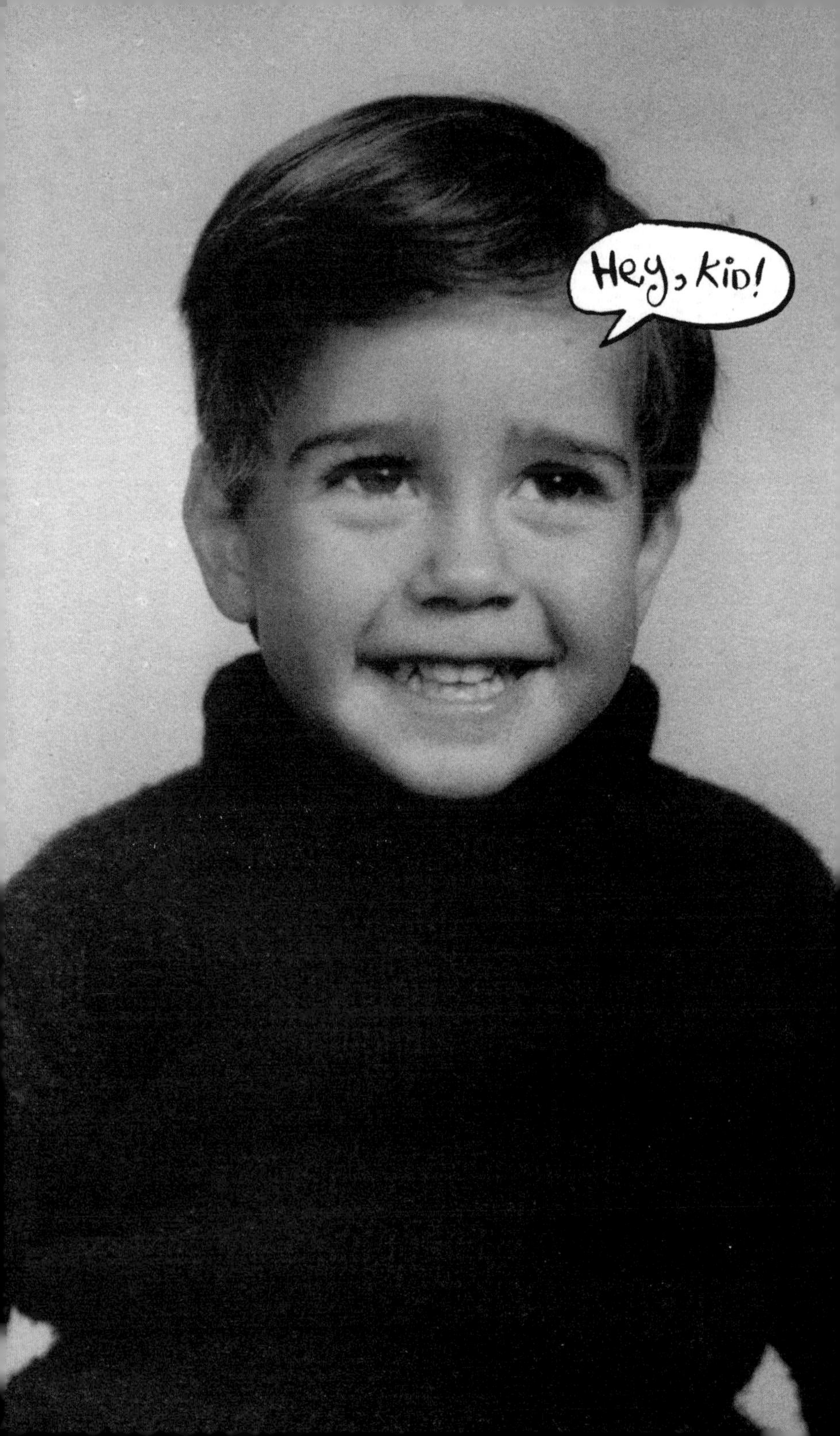
Hey, kid!

The
VOICE
in Your Head

I WROTE THIS BOOK FOR ME

I wrote this book for the same reason I've written more than a half dozen others. Because I wanted to read it and couldn't find it in my bookstore. A book about a creature that lives in my head.

Ever since I was fairly small, I've heard this little voice that provides a running narration for most of the things I do. It comments on my decisions, it tells me what other people were thinking about me, it points out bad things that might happen if I do one thing or another. And it hardly ever shuts up!

While this voice clearly lives in my head, I knew it wasn't really me. It didn't sound like me and it didn't help me. It limited me. It scared me. It kept me up at night. If this voice was me, it wasn't the me I wanted to be.

Eventually I started to look for ways to get away from this voice. Or at least to listen to it less. It may not be possible to completely turn it off forever but I just wanted it to matter less, to stay out of my way. As I grew older, the voice troubled me less about certain things and took up other causes instead. Instead of saying I was zitty, it called me wrinkled—that sort of thing. Clearly, the solution wasn't to wait it out. Instead I had to outwit it.

I started to poke around and I realized that every creative person I came across had the same sort of problem. In fact, most everyone with a mind did too. So if the voice is in every head and yet those heads manage to do incredible things like invent the iPhone, learn Italian, and have retrospectives at the Guggenheim, it is possible to fight this voice and win. Many people have.

So I did a lot of thinking and reading and talking to experts and I came to understand this voice and what it wanted. And I also learned how to avoid its influence ... well, most of the time.

Important confession: I will admit to you now, at the beginning of this book, while you still have time to find your receipt and return it to the bookstore, that I still occasionally fall victim to this voice. Even while I was writing these very pages, the voice intruded, stuck out a foot, distracted and almost sabotaged me several times. But, despite these setbacks, I do know, after all this searching, how to get past this powerful force and get on with my life. And I will share all I learned with you.

Together we'll unravel the causes of this pesky demon and the many ways it can affect you. Along the way, I will tell you about my own struggles with my inner critic. I'll also share some examples from the many, many people who have told me tales of their struggles.

And finally we'll get to the solutions—strategies that won't just shut down the voice in your head; they'll also help you to do great work, achieve your ambitions, and ultimately help make the world a better place.

The voice in your head is not evil, but it does evil.

It is powerful, but its power can be broken.

And now more than ever in the history of our brainy species, we need to take it on and prevent it from preventing us from addressing the many challenges our world faces today. I hope when we're done, you'll find these ideas and strategies useful. And if you don't, I hope you will write your own book and tell me where I can buy a copy.

PSSST!

Here you are, minding your own business.

Maybe you're gazing out the window, daydreaming about your future.

Or you're wandering through a bookstore, looking for inspiration to refocus your life.

Maybe you just got off the phone with your old school mate who told you he quit his job to start his own business.

Or you just got briefed on a new project at work and you're staring at the blank screen of your computer.

Or maybe it's 3 A.M. and you are just staring at the ceiling, much too wide awake.

Your attention shifts inward, to a spot behind your eyeballs.

A little voice starts up back there and it's murmuring, just to you.

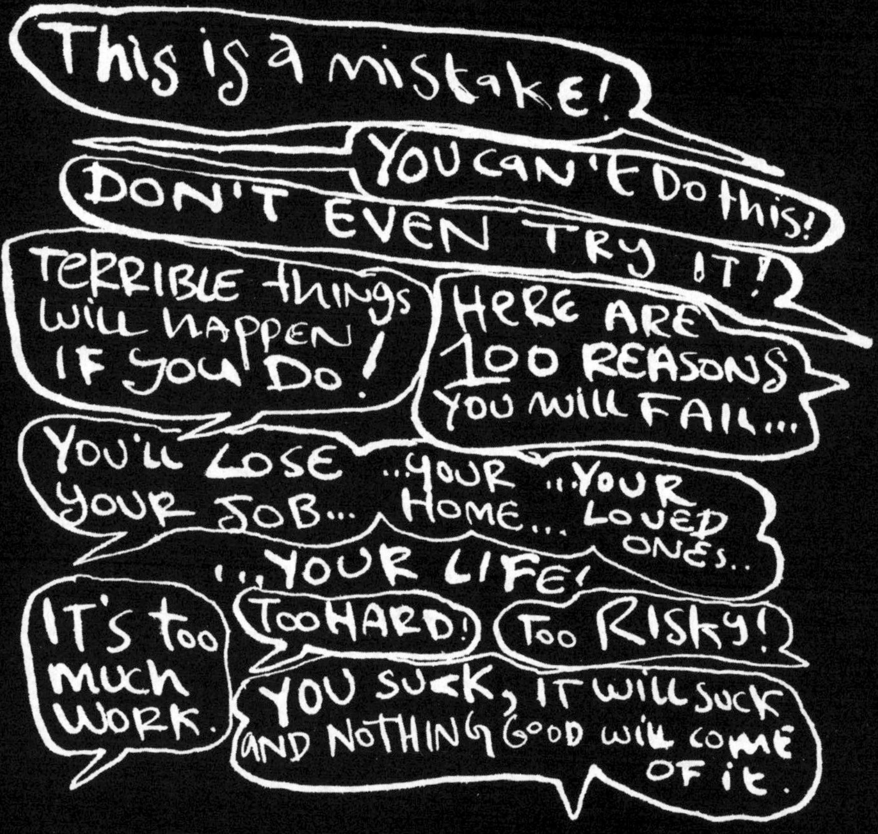
This is a mistake!
YOU can't Do this!
DON'T EVEN TRY IT!
TERRIBLE things WILL HAPPEN IF YOU DO!
HERE ARE 100 REASONS YOU WILL FAIL...
YOU'LL LOSE YOUR JOB... ...YOUR HOME... ...YOUR LOVED ONES.. ...YOUR LIFE!
IT'S too much WORK.
TOO HARD!
Too RISKY!
YOU SUCK, IT WILL SUCK AND NOTHING GOOD WILL COME OF it.

The voice is here to warn you that what you are doing—or thinking of doing, or just thinking about thinking about doing—is a terrible idea that will destroy your life. It tells you the dire consequences that are about to fall on you. How your life will unravel—maybe even end—if you take the step you are contemplating. It is here to worry you, to scare you, to stop you.

The voice makes you second-guess yourself. You can go from the verge of making a decision to backing away, to asking others' opinions, to questioning your judgment, to trashing everything you have ever accomplished, dismissing every bit of praise or encouragement you have ever received, doubting yourself to the core.

This voice uses more than just words. It messes with your body, your nerves, your sweat glands. It makes you physically anxious. It squirts adrenaline into your bloodstream, ties your guts in knots, releases butterflies to flop around your tummy, and gushes cold sweats down your pits and brow.

It knows you well. In fact, it sounds like a caring friend, concerned and just here to protect you from a horrible decision. It's a familiar old voice, one that's been whispering in your ear as far back as you can remember.

It's the voice of the inner critic, the opposition, the prosecutor, the worry wart. It's the voice of doom.

If you hear this voice, and I know you do, you're not crazy. You're not a loser. You're not alone. You're just human.

But despite how common this predicament is, it's also very damaging. The voice has the ability to limit your potential, crush your happiness and derail your dreams.

And we're going to stop it.

THE VOICE AND THE MAKER

More than anything, the voice messes with creative people. And in one way or another these days, most of us are involved with creativity. New ideas, new directions: these are the situations that make the voice jabber loudest. Why? Because the voice hates change and risk and whenever we rearrange the mental furniture of our lives, it freaks out. The voice fears the unknown and the different because they can't be controlled.

This is an important thing to remember: When the voice starts up, it's because you are trying to change something. And if you are going to be a functioning person on this ever-turning planet, you will have to eventually make change too. So to be happy (or even functional), you are going to have to learn to shut that voice down.

WHO AM I AND WHAT DO I KNOW?

Throughout this book, I am going to share stories from my own life and career to show how the voice can limit you—and how to shut it down.

I have been a creative person my whole life and people have been paying me to make things for over thirty years. I've been a copywriter, an author, an illustrator, a creative director, an advertising executive, and an entrepreneur. I have created many, many new ideas with millions of dollars at stake. I have had many briefings, deadlines, presentations, reviews, awards, and failures. I have spent lots of times staring at blank pages and empty screens, wrestling with that voice inside me. I've made some poor decisions, mismanaged relationships, limited and tortured myself—all because I listened to the voice when I should have known better.

I have also worked with lots of other people who have this same little voice ringing in their ears. I've collaborated with and managed hundreds of people who are paid to be creative too—art directors, copywriters, designers, producers, photographers, illustrators, directors, and editors. Every single one of them has faced this same problem, with varying degrees of success. I've seen it drive some people to limit or even sabotage their careers. I've seen it turn great potential into mediocrity. I've seen the voice make people misbehave, waste time and money, and lose clients. And I've worked with some people who used the voice to their advantage, spurring themselves on to new and greater creativity, solving big, important problems.

I've also been a teacher, helping people learn to discover and express their creativity. I have written books, led workshops and classes. And time and again, I've seen people beat themselves up before they even begin, muttering harsh judgments, ripping up work, cursing and threatening to quit. I've seen people leave art school, quit jobs, stop making their own art, and crush their dreams. And I've helped them to face those fears and turn them into positive, creative habits that have changed their lives.

Over the years, I have figured out how to overcome all the many damaging effects of this voice in our heads. I did it by studying the enemy, by dissecting the voice, its origins and causes. I have studied its behavior and strategies for monkeying with my mind. I have researched different techniques and discussed them with experts—artists, teachers, and psychologists. And I have discussed these ideas with lots of frustrated creative people—and have seen how these techniques can bring them relief and new direction.

Helping win this struggle is particularly important to me because I feel creative people have the power to save the world. The human race faces so many challenges these days, but we also have so many new tools to solve them. The idea that some stupid, nattering voice in our heads might stop us from creating solutions is scary. So let's silence that voice and get to work!

THE INCESSANT NARRATOR

First, we need to spend some time understanding the voice in our heads. After all, it plays a big role in our lives, narrating every minute of every day. Most of the time we aren't paying it much attention, but it's still in there, narrating the story of our lives, giving play-by-play commentary on every move we make. So we need to isolate it and pin a mic on it to understand what it is saying and why.

ANGIE'S MONKEY TALE: Angie is the mother of three young boys. She recently took an art class and started creating for the first time since she was a kid herself. As soon as her kids took a nap, she sat down to draw and the voice woke up: "But you should be cleaning. When the kids are awake, you need to be spending time with them. You only have a year off, and then you go back to work. Don't waste this year making drawings no one will ever care about. You should start supper. You should organize the toy room. You should go pay bills. You should wash the sticky floors." She told me, "There are always a million 'shoulds' that the voice can throw at me. And sure, I hear all the people that say I need to take time for myself. That I should take some time to do what makes me happy. That I will be a better mother. The problem is, this voice, the one yelling at me, is so much louder."

LISTEN TO THE VOICE

So what does it sound like? Listen to it for a minute and pay attention just to the quality of its voice. It shouldn't be hard to hear. I'm sure that as you read this book, the voice is very noisy and complaining. It doesn't like to be discussed and scrutinized and much prefers that the focus stay on you and your many flaws. But let's ignore the protests for now and concentrate instead on the style of the voice.

Does it whisper? Does it have an accent? Does it sing? Does it echo? How old does it sound? Is it high-pitched or low-? Does it sit right against your ear or is it deep in your head?

Now, try to put a body and a face to that voice. Make it a creature.

How big is it? What does it smell like? How does it move? Is it an animal? Is it a demon? Is it a bank of fog or a chorus of mice?

I imagine it looks a bit like Gollum.

It's whiny and creepy and lives back in the dark cave of my skull. It never rests and has big, glowing eyes that constantly dart around in fear. It has a mouthful of sharp little teeth to nip at the edges of my mind and it smells musty, of cold sweat and old fish. So, like Gollum . . . but meatier and covered in grey-brown fur that's fairly oily, like an unwashed mutt.

I call this lovely thing "the Monkey." It jabbers and hoots like a monkey and it smells like one too. Only worse.

Maybe my picture fits your creature too. If not, just substitute your species in for the rest of the descriptions I'll give you. I'm pretty sure they'll still fit whether you imagine you're carrying around a snake or a gargoyle, a gremlin or a gopher with a chainsaw.

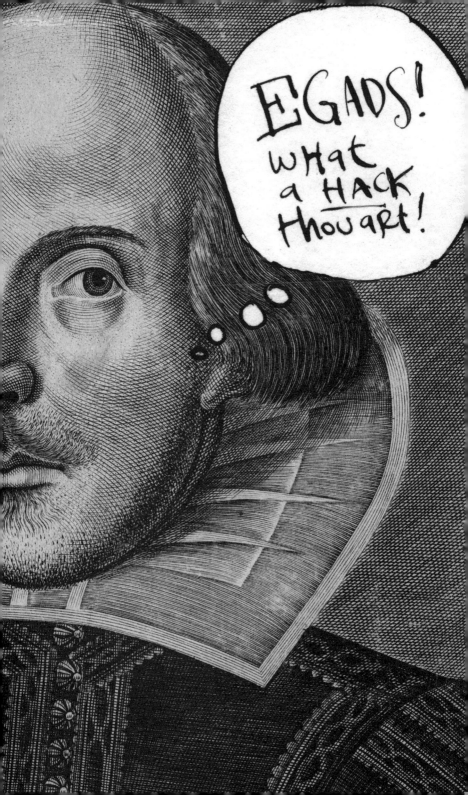

ONLY PSYCHOS NEVER WONDER IF THEY'RE NUTS

The only people who don't have monkeys camping out in their heads are sociopaths. Literally, they are the people who were somehow raised with no guilt, no risk aversion, no brakes . . . no monkey. The rest of us—Bill Gates, Lady Gaga, Gandhi—we all live with the monkey glowering at the back of the cave, driving us crazy now and then. So don't worry, there are six billion of us hosting the monkey; you're in good company.

Every successful creative person goes through periods when they fear they are frauds. That they have somehow conned the world into thinking that they are any good. And that any minute, the knock is going to come on the door. They can't imagine that the truly great people struggle as much as they do. Or they worry it's all too easy, that this success must be some sort of devil's bargain which will be stripped from them at any moment. It's normal to fear success. When you stop worrying, you become a pompous windbag with an over-inflated ego. Then your standards slip, and you slide down the slick slope to suckdom.

RUTH ANN'S MONKEY: "Her name is Mabel Anderson and in my imagination she looks like this: a librarian, middle-aged. She wears cardigan sweaters buttoned up over Peter Pan–collared blouses, tweed skirts, thick hose, and sensible lace-up shoes. Her hair is pulled back in a bun with a pencil stuck in it. She showed up one day as I was attempting to make some art, whispering in my ear, 'Dearie, you really don't have any talent. You really don't want anyone to see that. That would really be bad for your self-esteem.' What I really wanted her to do was shut up and leave me alone."

Meet
Your
MONKEY

KELLY'S MONKEY TALE: Kelly's monkey is relentless. "When I'm at work, the monkey mind chitters about how I have nothing worthy of saying. If what I do say doesn't fit with the conversation, or it doesn't make sense to someone, it tells me it was right. That I'm stupid, and that I don't belong there." Kelly's passion is to be a writer and she has taken many classes and worked hard to perfect her craft. "The monkey mind tells me I'm wasting my time. That I should just accept things as they are. That I don't know enough people, that no one likes me anyway. That I'd never manage to convince someone to buy one book, never mind enough books to make it a sustainable business." At the end of a yoga class, as the instructor guided the students through a relaxation exercise, her monkey whispered: "You know you're only here so that someone will touch you." Kelly started to well up, then desperately tried to distract herself so that when the lights went up, she wasn't sitting there, sobbing.

YOUR OWN WORST ENEMY

The monkey is a formidable foe.

It is more devious than you and it has plenty of time on its hands. It is there 24/7, waiting and watching for you to make a move, to even contemplate a move, and it is ready to trip you up. It can use everything you know against you, push every button, pull every lever—and it is unrelenting. It has the keys to the file room and knows the combination of the vault in your skull. Don't let that get you down. But don't underestimate it either.

MONKEY IN THE MIDDLE

The monkey has opinions about most things. It's a busy little voice and it can think of a good reason to be afraid of most decisions, of any impending event, big or small. It can give you umpteen reasons to do something tomorrow instead of today; to ask for more and more people's opinions before you make a move; can tell you what that stranger at the cocktail party will reply if you say hi.

That Zit could be a TUMOR. The pilot's probably DRUNK. That Girl's too hot for you. Do you smell smoke?

EZGI'S MONKEY TALE: Ezgi is a freelance writer from Istanbul who has been wrestling with her monkey her whole adult life. "I started to see 'it' as a grumpy old lady. She likes to poke me with the needle in her hand and is really good at knowing what my soft spot is. She makes impressive entrances in the beginning of projects and says things like 'You are just seeking attention like a little girl. That's why you write. You're insincere. And these ideas are no good. You were never good at finding ideas anyway.' When I remind her of my past achievements, she answers, 'You might fool people once or twice, but this is not the case this time.' She never forgets to pay a visit to me after a rejection. Whenever an editor responds to me with 'No,' she screams back 'No! No! No!' while dancing. She crows, 'I told you so! I told you so! What were you thinking, sending your childish story to this prestigious magazine?' She hurts me mercilessly, but never forgets to remind me her intentions are all good. She says, 'I may sound harsh but I just don't want to see you suffering, honey.' Somehow I doubt it."

THE LIFE AND DEATH OF THE PROJECT

Through all my years in advertising, the monkey came along for the ride, contributing something unhelpful to every step of the creative process. I'll take you through one of my typical projects, complete with monkey annotation. See if it sounds familiar.

Every project begins with a briefing session. All of the creatives file into the conference room carrying pads and pens and Thermos cups of coffee. The strategist and account executives sit by the screen, rearranging their PowerPoint slides. The strategic brief appears onscreen, outlining the target, the objective, the strategy, and the various client deliverables. The monkey pulls up the Aeron chair next to me, ready to narrate.

This brief is absurd.
This project makes no sense.
Has anyone thought this through?
Nobody could solve this problem.
This product sucks the big one.

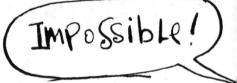

After the meeting, I sit down to work in my office and the commentary continues. But now, instead of just being critical, the monkey tries to distract me.

Hey, we have plenty of time 'til this is due.
Open your browser.
Wait, check out Facebook.
I'm hungry and I have to pee.
Let's go to lunch.

Then when I start to come up with ideas, it takes a different approach.

I don't know, that idea seems sort of weird.
Hasn't that been done already?
Can't you come up with anything original?

HaCK!

And just because I've left the office and gone home, the monkey keeps working. It'll wake me up in the middle of the night.

$5 FOOTLONG.

Well, I guess you still haven't thought
of anything.
Deadline's approaching.
What if you never think of
another idea?
What if this is the last assign-
ment they ever give you?
I see they are hiring at Subway.

Weeks pass and we're finally ready to present. As I start to set up our ideas, I hear the voice in the background.

Meh, I don't think they like it.
Whoa, I totally don't think they under-
stand it.
Ho! Look at that look on that one's face.
You better go back and explain that again.
I think your fly is open.

THeY HATE it YOU!

And after the presentation, after everybody's congratulating us on how great our work is, the monkey whispers in my ear:

Dude, you'll never come up with anything this good again.

I've been going to creative briefings for three decades and it gets easier—but not easy. Nonetheless, I have never not had an idea at all, never not come through. Dozens of times each year, year after year. The key? Practice. Experience. Perseverance. Head down. I don't always win each creative shoot-out, but I'm not afraid to glove up.

I'm sure you have the same sort of track record, no matter how many obstacles the monkey's kicked in your way. Try to remind yourself of that next time the monkey-go-round starts up.

MONKEY SUBSPECIES

You'll find that, while you have basically one monkey, it wears many masks.

THE BLUNDERER: You can't do this. Don't even try. You will fail. Don't humiliate yourself. You suck.

THE NITPICKER: Here's a long list of all the things you screwed up. They all matter equally. If this isn't 100% perfect, it utterly sucks.

THE FAKE: You are a fraud and an impostor. Everyone knows you can't do this. They're all laughing behind your naive back, you lying fool.

THE PARANOID: They're laughing and sneering, because no one likes you. Or trusts you. Or admires you. Or could ever love you. And they can't wait to see you screw up.

THE HOLY MONKEY: You are sinful and childish, have no self-control, and think only of yourself.

THE GOSSIP: Look at what idiots everyone else is. Imagine what they are saying about you.

THE WORRIER: Look, just be anxious. Because if you worry about absolutely everything, at least you are prepared for the inevitable disaster.

THE LUG: Let's forget it. Come curl up in a ball on the couch, watch *Judge Judy*, and empty another quart of Chunky Monkey ice cream.

THE CHEAP CHIMP: You will soon be broke. And homeless.

DR. MONKEY: And dead. You have been totally ignoring all the horrible diseases rampaging around inside you. And you don't floss enough.

THE UTOPIAN: Your life could be so perfect, so much better than this, if only you would listen to me. Instead, it sucks. As do you.

THE BLACK HOLE: *(Emits a deep, dark, silent, soul-sucking creative void broken by a throbbing alarm blaring, "Warning! You'll never achieve anything again, ever.")*

THE FUGGEDABOUT-IT: Tomorrow's another day. So's the day after next Thursday.

THE TIGER MOM-KEY: You will never live up to your potential and you'll bring us nothing but shame.

BEHAVE LIKE A MONKEY

The monkey can make you behave a bit like a monkey yourself.

If you find yourself quarreling with others and venting emotion inappropriately, chances are that you're not working, not creating, not thinking, not doing. Or alternatively, you may find yourself overworking, nights and weekends (on projects fueled by drudgery and obligation, not passion), living out of balance, out of harmony, out of fast food containers, far from your true self.

In my career as a creative director, I've run into a lot of people who are driven to melodramatics by their monkey puppeteers. They act out. Client questions your decision? Throw a fit. Need to cover up a blunder? The best defense is a good serving of self-righteous indignation. They're always drawing attention to themselves, making excuses, being prima donnas, making outrageous demands. A bigger office, a longer title, no brown M&Ms in the dressing room!

In the short run, this strategy might shift things your way. But eventually, instead of being famous for making things, you'll be notorious as a dysfunctional basket-case.

MARTHA

I knew a copywriter who'd spend the weeks after a briefing very busy, complaining. Her name was Martha. She'd say:

> "We need a lot more information. When is the deadline? That's ridiculous. We're far too busy already! Do they expect me to do this all by myself?"

And if we briefed other teams too, Martha would say,

> "Why are they working on my project? I'm not going to compete with these people! It's a waste of my time. I should just walk out of the room. I DESERVE RESPECT!"

Then the night before the assignment was due, Martha would get to work and . . . she'd have to stay up all night. Sometimes her ideas were great, often they weren't. Then she would complain about how tired and overworked she was, or how bad the brief or the product were.

Martha and the monkey managed to protect her with a thick layer of complaints. Despite all the good work that she (occasionally) did, Martha was part of the very next round of layoffs. Her monkey kept its job.

SICK AS A MONKEY

The monkey doesn't want what's good for you. He wants you slow and weak and distracted so he can have his way. A popular monkey game is monkeying with your health—mental and physical.

Am I unproductive because I am depressed? Or is the other way around? I should get that mole checked.

My tooth! My stomach! My back!

my hypochondria is in remission.

Get busy making something and see what happens to your mood. When I wake up at 3 A.M. with the ape chattering in my ear, I can only take so much lying there in the darkness. So I crawl out of bed, go to my desk and draw or write something, anything. It's a miracle cure. My back won't hurt, my allergies will recede, my bank account will get in balance. My mind is eased, the chimp goes back to sleep and so do I.

MONKEY ON YOUR BACK

Why do rock stars overdose? The monkey.

What happened to Tiger Woods and Michael Jackson? The monkey.

THE MONKEY LOVES **FRENCH FRIES** AND BUZZFEED. DRINKING. CHOCOLATE CAKE. INSOMNIA. SCIATICA. REAL HOUSEWIVES.

Anything that fills the hole that comes from **NOT DOING** what your true passion calls for.

DOOM

The monkey doesn't like new things. It doesn't like change. It is always worried—especially about things that haven't even happened yet.

That's why it excels at pointing out the dark clouds on the horizon. It can show you the most far-fetched possibilities, how a scaffold could collapse on your head, a taxi could ride up on the sidewalk, a pigeon could crap on your lunch if you don't eat at your desk. It has you up at night worrying through every scenario, trussing yourself up with belt and suspenders, an umbrella, a raincoat, galoshes, and a lightning rod.

Worry and fear are the best ways to protect yourself. Hunker down, stay put, shut up.

THE MONKEY MOVES THE GOAL POSTS

It's dangerous taking advice from the monkey, and not just because its advice is often terrible.

Its convictions may sound rock-solid, but the monkey will switch sides in a hot second if it will rattle your cage.

It can say you're not good enough—or too good.

Lazy or a workaholic.

Too pushy or too laid back.

It can say you should settle for the easy way out—or that you always refuse to go the extra mile.

The monkey will tell you exactly what your life should be like. And then it'll show you how incredibly far your life is from this perfection.

If you say, "Okay, I'll change. I'll get a new job, new haircut, new gym, new attitude . . ." the vision that the monkey holds out will slowly change, showing it's a mirage you can never achieve.

TAKE THE RED PILL

The monkey likes steady, reliable habits. It wants to program you so you always respond the same way, no matter whether it's appropriate or not, in your best interests or not.

MEET A STRANGER

YOUR BOSS CALLS

E-MAIL ARRIVES

TRAFFIC SLOWS

It's like *The Matrix*. These habits mean you aren't reacting to what is actually going on now but to an illusion, a mental construct, a program. Your mind is on automatic. Your imagination is handcuffed.

How do you develop fresh, creative ideas if your mindset is utterly formulaic?

How do you create delight or surprise if you can't actually feel it, if the monkey tells you exactly how things are going to turn out every time?

How can you avoid being disengaged and bored if you always react in the same predictable way?

How can you grow if your behaviors and attitudes were formed to respond to problems and situations that no longer exist?

How can you be happy if you are swimming down a deep rut full of concrete?

We live in a rapidly changing world; you've got to be engaged and responsive. Old tricks won't cut it.

BARBARA'S MONKEY TALE: "I could spend my entire day drawing, painting, writing, creating. Everything I look at stimulates my imagination and inspires creative ideas inside my head. But my critic never stops reminding me that I should be doing something more constructive and less selfish than playing around in the arts. I want to write a children's book, teach journaling classes to friends who have voiced interest, market my necklaces, sell my journals, paint large-scale cows, but something stops me. My critic tells me that I have no imagination, that if I was good it would come more naturally. The monkey has defeated me over the years. I've had plenty of opportunities to market myself, but I haven't . . . I think it's fear . . . of what I don't know. Stupid monkey."

ONE *MORE* THING...

The monkey will always find you one more reason to delay. Do more research. Ask others' opinions. Find an agent, find a publisher, get a contract, get a new desk chair. Or maybe we should just go out for a doughnut? ... It can be never-ending. That's okay with the monkey. It has endless time. But you don't.

All this activity makes it seem like you are doing something, but truly you're not. You're just frittering away time and defeating your creative impulse with thoughts of fine art, chocolate, naps, sex ... The illusion of productivity is the bone the monkey throws you.

JOE'S MONKEY TALE: Joe is an illustrator. But he'd really love to paint. He told me: "My problem is always: Can I 'justify' doing a painting right now when there are still other things on my to-do list?" Recently, Joe ordered some really nice oil-primed Belgian linen canvas, set up his oil paints and his favorite brushes. But months went by and he couldn't begin. The monkey always managed to come up with something to shunt painting down the list. He had chores. Someone needed his help. An assignment came up. And slowly his canvas and brushes gather dust and "My monkey just sits around asking: How can you justify painting when you still have to _____ (fill in the blank)?"

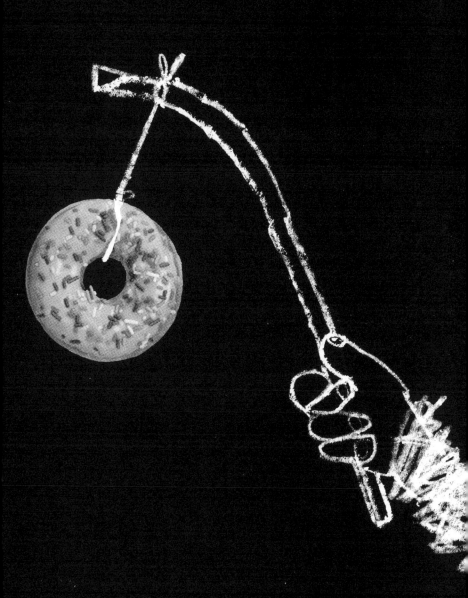

PERFECT IS THE ENEMY OF DONE

At first glance, perfectionism doesn't seem like one of the monkey's tricks. After all, it's not unreasonable to want to do things well, to have high standards, to do your best. The problem is that the monkey insists you do everything perfectly. Not just your job or your art, but your laundry, your parallel parking, your push-ups. It can insist that you letter the address on a UPS package perfectly, search for two hours for the perfect way to cook a burger, line up the pens on your desk in perfect lines, be the last one to leave the office.

But no matter how high your standards, the monkey will still make sure perfection is always just out of reach. As your ideas begin to bubble to the surface, the monkey insists on judging right away, pointing out how far below perfection you have fallen. The paint's not dry and it's already adding its fingerprints. Even though you know most ideas don't hatch without some room for improvement, the monkey can make you sling them on the trash pile before they catch their first breath. It evaluates your idea, then your tools, your execution, the words others use to evaluate it, the long-term potential, on and on.

It'll point out where the idea misses the brief, that someone irrelevant to the process might dislike it, that it might not be original, that it is beyond the budget. All of these judgments are premature because they can be addressed with work and thought, but the monkey won't give you a chance. Soon you are wrung out. You feel beleaguered by all this criticism, overwhelmed by the feeling that all of your ideas are going to be deficient.

The fact is, insisting on perfection is just another form of hubris. It's predicated on the assumption that somehow you can meet standards that are way too high for the average person, that while others might accept something subpar, you insist on it being done just so. And then you (and the monkey) beat yourself up when it's revealed that you too are simply human.

Here's the dirty secret:

PERFECTIONISTS ARE NOT MORE PRODUCTIVE THAN PEOPLE WHO AREN'T CRAZED, OBSESSIVE, WORKAHOLIC NITPICKERS.

Often the opposite.

When your priorities are askew and you get overly obsessed with incidental details, it's a lot harder to do what needs to be done. Be a bit more realistic about your capabilities and your priorities. Accept that in most cases, good enough is just perfect.

A NEAT STALL IS A SIGN OF A DEAD HORSE

What happens when you're so fixated on perfection that you never begin? Never begin writing. Never begin making stuff. Never begin pursuing any sort of passion for fear of not being able to do it incredibly well. Nothing you do will be good enough—even for you. Why bother if you can't be great?

A variation is fiddliness. Constant reappraisal, erasing, tweaking, reconsidering, seeking more opinions, on and on. Never done, never good enough.

One of the problems with perfectionism is that you think you can conceive the destination before you embark on the journey, that you can plan it all out in advance, and that nothing else can intrude and change the outcome you have conceived. But the world doesn't work that way; unless you are doing something extremely simple and banal, something you can actually hold in your brain all at once, it will invariably intrude and change your well-laid plans. And, secondly, you should welcome that intrusion. The accidents, mistakes, serendipities and ink splatters that the universe throws in your path make you and your life more interesting. Perfection isn't natural. It can be constipated and inert.

Meanwhile, if you are waiting to make stuff because you haven't got the perfect pen or paper or subject or teacher or block of time . . . get over it. We all make shit every day. If we didn't, we'd die. Or at least be really cranky.

PERFECTION AIN'T SO PERFECT

Perfection seems like the goal. It's impressive to see all the pressure and stress perfectionists put on themselves. It seems like they are working on a higher order. But maybe they are just frozen by their monkeys. Focused myopically on perfectionism rather than the goal of the project. Perfection causes paraplegia because you've forgotten that it's not perfection you need. It's a solution that works.

Perfection is hard to achieve and always impermanent. The exact right solution for a given time will always wear out its perfection. Otherwise we wouldn't have evolution—empires wouldn't crumble, champions wouldn't fall, dinosaurs wouldn't become, well, dinosaurs. The universe is always in flux, so waiting endlessly for perfection just means you'll miss the boat.

JANE'S MONKEY TALE: Often, Jane gets inspired to put pen to paper and brush to paint. "But then my monkey kicks me right up the butt." Jane says, "It tells me I need to have everything perfect before I can even start to think about putting something down on paper. I research, research and keep researching . . . so that I know which are the best papers to use, the best watercolors with the best pigments, the most vibrant colors, the best brushes, pens, fountain pens, inks; then I start buying them, then I look at online videos to see how to paint, but before I paint I need to know how to sketch so I start researching again and again and again. And I rarely put anything down on paper. Because when I try to, I find it difficult to breathe and I want to cry. I want to be Picasso, or nothing at all. How flaming egotistical!"

EVEN THE *MONA LISA* HAS CRACKS

What the monkey says can seem like Truth, a deep, dark truth only you and the monkey know about. It seems like it knows you better than anyone ever could—warts, zits, pockmarks and all; what you look like naked and a few pounds overweight.

This intimacy can be mistaken for insight and fact—but what if it's just coming from the crotchety neighbor who peeks under your blinds? What if the monkey only sees one meager side of you and extrapolates, bizarrely, mistakenly, the rest. And maybe you've lost quite a few pounds since last he peeked, maybe you've stopped picking your nose, maybe you only scratched your butt that one time . . . maybe the imperfections the monkey is picking on are just the dust bunnies under the throne in a gorgeous, gleaming palace that is You. And so what? Maybe you are just a flawed (but minorly flawed) major masterpiece.

ROSEMARY'S MONKEY TALE: At art school, Rosemary was assigned to copy an Old Master. "I chose Vermeer. Because I love Vermeer. Needless to say, I struggled with the painting and was so disappointed that I couldn't make my painting look like the Vermeer painting. I was so discouraged that instead of working harder, I stopped painting. I can't paint like Vermeer! It was only years later when I returned to painting that I had the brainstorm idea that NO ONE CAN PAINT LIKE VERMEER! Not even his contemporaries. That's what set him apart. Now I teach art workshops to beginners and I tell them that story. And I remind them that you can only be as good as you are this very day. That you can't expect your work to look like someone who has been doing it for years. I stress the fact that the more they do it the better they will get. I give them permission for their work not to be perfect and they embrace that! It's amazing but true."

ADAPTATION

This book may give you a lot of things to think about. But don't. Don't think about these concepts in too much depth. Don't analyze them and dissect them. Don't make rules about how you will be from now. Don't set up new expectations. Don't try to twist yourself in a new direction. Untwist yourself, and just *be* instead.

Trust that the real you, the inner you, will hear these ideas and know how things really are. Let these ideas work on a subconscious level while you get back to work.

Stop thinking about yourself. Stop fretting. Stop doubting. Stop trying to rationalize your way through this. Stop trying to change things before you can start work. Trust in your ability to adapt to what happens and still be fine. Better than fine.

You are creative and a problem-solver. You are resilient—and you will survive. That's called evolution. You adapt to what comes up and in ways you can't yet imagine. Things may not go the way you planned them to go. They may be utterly different. Unimaginably so. You can't control it. But you can still be perfectly . . . happy. Go with the flow and respond when it happens.

Choose to be more evolved than your monkey.

What Does

Your

MONKEY

Want?

THE MISSING LINK

So—what is this monkey voice? Where does it come from? What does it want? What banana can we toss it so it will shut up and go away?

I used to suppose that the monkey was some person in my past, someone who had so impacted me that their voice still echoed in my skull and would forever more. Perhaps it was my woodshop teacher from sixth grade. Or maybe it was my second stepfather. Or the sneering, sing-song voice of the bully that cracked open my head with a rock when I was eleven. Or a kid I knew in high school who was way cooler than almost all of us. Or maybe it was your voice—maybe that was the real reason you came here today, to tell me how much this book sucks.

But it turns out it's simpler. It's all of these voices—and none of them. It's one you know much better. It's the voice that's editing this sentence as I write it. It's critiquing my typing skills. It's correcting my posture. It's wondering why you aren't working right now, or going to the gym, or calling your mother—instead of reading some book.

It's the hard-wired, deep-dyed voice of fear.

MONKEY BRAIN

Buried deep in your head, at the base of your skull, lies the original chunk of your brain on top of which all the good human bits are layered. The tough little core is the amygdala, the monkey brain, that protects us from attack. If something new and different enters our environment, this part of the brain is the first response. The hairs on your arms and neck stand up on end, your lips pull back to bare your teeth, your heart rate raises, adrenaline surges through your arms.

This first line of defense assumes that new=bad. When I walk my two miniature dachshunds, they are under the misimpression that they are out there not to do their business but to protect me from every strange dog that passes our way. They can sense an invader from two blocks away— their hackles go up and low growls rumble in their chests. As the stranger approaches, they sharpen their toenails on the sidewalk, pull back their ears, and bare their teeth. If a truck slams on its brakes or a door slams, they yank in their tails and run as fast as possible in the opposite direction. Once at safe distance, they will spin around and bark violently at the offender, announcing that they aren't actually cowards and are now ready for battle.

The monkey brain says 'fight or flight'. It provokes a mindless response that could save your skin if you were living in the wild surrounded by scary beasts. If you are in a conference room, that response may be a little over the top. Nonetheless, that alarm system is sitting deep in there, ready to blow the klaxons at every new idea. It's our job to yank on its leash or distract it with a whistle.

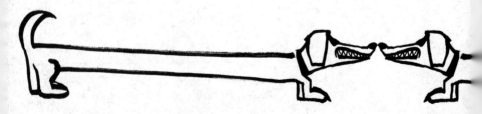

YOU'LL PUT YOUR EYE OUT WITH THAT

It doesn't seem fair. The amygdala could just lie dormant like your appendix or an old pay phone. After all, it was built to stave off attacks that are long gone, saber-tooths and what not. But the monkey voice still sees threats all around because it was told that they are out there, all around. And told recently, just a few decades ago. The monkey speaks in a familiar voice—because it's the voice you grew up with.

All parents tell their children these things for their own good. To protect them from harm. To protect them from eating insects, swallowing safety pins, and playing in traffic. They say things in an exaggerated, emphatic way so these lessons will get through their children's thick heads. It makes sense. Parents want their children to avoid risk so that they will survive.

Eventually you internalize these voices. Or you become a juvenile delinquent. Or you don't listen, you fall off a roof and die, then you're out of the gene pool. The monkey goes from being an outside voice to being a voice inside.

THE MONKEY IN THE FAMILY TREE

The monkey parrots back warnings you received as a child. But, even more insidious, it dredges up fears that may not even be related to your own life, fears from previous generations, many steps removed. The deprivations, the threats of a bygone era haunt them still and were probably passed down to you. But as they were transmitted, they were magnified, abstracted and distorted too.

When my 97-year-old neighbor died, we helped his kids empty out the house he'd lived in since the 1960s. The basement was filled with shelf after shelf of canned goods, many so old they'd rusted and lost their labels. He had hoarded all this food just in case the Great Depression he lived through as a young man suddenly came back. He was ready for a Soviet nuclear attack too, with a rack of radiation suits, gas masks, and a rifle or two.

My neighbor may have been obsessive about the return of Armageddon, but he passed on deep, insistent fears to his kids. One became a hoarder too, accumulating all sorts of crap without really understanding why it seemed so important to her. Another daughter rebelled and led a brutally pared-down life, refusing to put down roots, renting a different apartment in a new city each year, furnished only with a mattress on the floor and some borrowed chairs. Each kid received a monkey that was born on a bread line and, 75 years later, still fretted about famine ahead.

TALENT MAY BE INHERITED; SO ARE MONKEYS

If someone in your family had to give up their dreams, maybe their creative ambitions, that sacrifice could come back to haunt you too.

Did you never overhear your dad telling your mother, "I'm not paying for some painting class. We shouldn't encourage her. No one makes a living as an artist." Maybe he'd wanted to go to art school but wasn't supported by your grandfather and had to become an accountant, so he spent your childhood channeling his pain into squashing your creativity. Maybe your mom got pregnant too early and had to go work at the DMV instead of writing that novel. Maybe your great-grandfather became a baker instead of a sculptor. Who knows; it's all back there in the shadowy past and it has controlled and shaped the way your family sees the world ever since.

You can prove your legacy wrong. That following your dream won't land you out on the street cadging change from strangers. That the Dust Bowl is over, the mortgage crisis is past, 9/11 is history, and that you would rather deal with new, actual crises when they come up (if you have to) than relive ones long gone. There's an old military cliché, that each generation of generals tries to fight the last war rather than the present one, and that goes double for the monkey and his army of tired, dusty skeletons.

Time for a fresh start that's bright and creative.

MIDNIGHT AT THE OASIS

When I was eleven, my art teacher gave us an assignment: Draw birds. I spent the weekend drawing a huge picture of an oasis surrounded by trees, all filled with birds of every feather. Swans and ducks in the water, ravens and pigeons and robins in the trees, hawks overhead, sparrows on the ground. I carried it proudly to school and placed on the pile on the teacher's desk. This was my best drawing ever!

The following week, I got the piece back. On the back of the drawing, the teacher had written : "The assignment was birds, not landscape. D+."

This teacher also taught woodshop and coached soccer. Maybe he hated having to teach kids drawing. Maybe his dad wanted him to be a mechanical engineer. Maybe he'd had a fight with his wife. Maybe his team had lost. Whatever it was, he unwittingly stabbed me in the heart with his red pencil that day. He handed the monkey a new script: "You are nothing special, you do not belong here."

Did you ever hear an external voice that the monkey recorded and now plays back, heading you off at a creative crossroads?

Was it the first art teacher who said something casual and cruel:

"Remember, most people don't have talent. I'm sure you're good at something."

Was it the dean of the art school who rejected your application?

The first boss who killed all of your favorite ideas?

An article about the percentage of art school grads who now work at Starbucks?

These are old voices, maybe even the voices of dead people, talking about old, vanished problems. Why must they still echo in your head?

VANESSA'S MONKEY TALE: In high school, Vanessa's monkey convinced her to stop making art. In college, it stopped her creative writing. Then, at 25, Vanessa was diagnosed with very aggressive non-Hodgkin's lymphoma. She was told to to ditch all sugary foods, become vegan and only buy products from Whole Foods. When she was unable to afford or adhere to all the restrictions, her monkey said, "You're doing cancer wrong!" In response, Vanessa started crocheting lymph nodes with funny faces on them and gave them to her nurses and then to other cancer surviors. Demand was so high, she started a business. "Now that I'm closing in on 30, I'm learning that my monkey is trying to protect me from feeling hurt, humiliated or ashamed. It's just going about it in an awful way."

LIVING IN THE REAL WORLD

Things that happened long ago were real. The pain was real. The marks were real. As we grew bigger, other bad things happened. Unimaginable things. Things that were also all too real.

But the worst things seem to be the things that could be.

The sound of approaching sirens that could be heading to your house.

The boss who could be getting ready to fire you.

The smell that could be smoke.

The leading indicators that could be a sign.

The cough from your child's room.

The phone ringing in the night.

The falling buildings.

The impending war.

The news around the clock.

Bad things happen. But worse things *could*. What does happen can be cleaned up or treated or paid for or even buried. But what *could* happen must only be dealt with one way. By refusing to fear what could be. By accepting that all that matters is all that is. That no matter how bad it is, we will live with it. That the world that skulks out of the midnight recesses of your head is just your creation. And that you can put your imagination to better use. And insist on living only in what is.

IT'S DEJA VU ALL OVER AGAIN

Whatever voice you're hearing, it's just a specter. Whatever sword carved the scars into your psyche, you have the power to move past it. As grownups, we have the ability to see that the affronts and critiques of the past are just puffs of air that have long since dissipated. Only we carry them forward. We re-record them onto the deepest wrinkles of our brains, keeping them alive year after year.

LP

to cassette

to CD

to MP3

to Spotify

. . . Same old song.

Every single cell in your body is replaced every seven years. You are a completely new being from cerebellum to big toenails. You have the power to override the rewrite, to define these ancient wounds as irrelevancies that do not bear on the wonderful creature you are today, a creative adult with great strength and potential.

CREATIVITY

and the

Monkey

WHY THE MONKEY HATES CREATIVITY

Here's the big question: Why do creative things make the monkey screech the loudest? (Because they do, you know.)

It all starts early: Remember, the monkey is the thoughts and rules that protected you when you were little. If it's new—it's unknown. And it could be deadly.

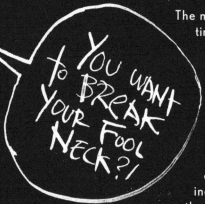

The monkey protected us at the dawn of time when all around lurked threats and danger. But saber-tooths are gone.

Creative people are all about change and risk and novelty and the unknown. That's our business. We create new solutions. We rock the boat. We subvert the status quo. We embrace the unknown. And as change is unleashed, creative people inevitably become the embodiment of the risk and the target of the fear.

Change can feel like wildfire. Change one thing, and soon change can engulf everything. Our jobs, our security, our very lives. Creativity endangers our prior assumptions. It courts disapproval. It invites rejection. That's why creative work attracts questions, criticism, even attack. Creative work puts us out there. It isolates us on the center stage. It invites the threat of being misunderstood on a fundamental level: I don't get it. Therefore, I don't get you.

But we are on the side of right. The side of progress. Change is inevitable. You just have to roll with it and embrace it—or be its lunch.

THE DANGER OF FEELING

Not only does the monkey target creative people but creative folks make great targets.

Creative people notice more.

Creative people think more.

Creative people are comfortable with their imaginations.

Creative people feel more deeply.

All these things mean we fear more too. We hear danger on the horizon before anyone else does. We can imagine its impact more acutely. We can imagine every possible disaster scenario.

We live with change. We feel its rumble first. And what we create makes people uncomfortable and scared and jealous and angry, and so we become the obvious target. Remind yourself: It's not you, it's them—and their monkeys.

What you are doing matters. And that's why it's under attack.

WHEN MONKEYS RIDE DINOSAURS

At my first job in advertising, I had the responsibility of setting up the projector when we had a new business meeting. Our reel of commercials was literally that, a big spool of 16 mm film. It seemed pretty cool. A few years later, every conference room sported a ¾" videotape deck and our reels were on tapes the size of a Stephen King novel. Soon we just slipped in a DVD. And then in the last few years, all our work was digitized and we played it in a browser window.

But none of these seemingly revolutionary changes were the really meaningful one.

While we were all tinkering with the latest gizmos, few saw the real sea change approaching: that the whole business of making TV commercials would eventually end up in hospice, undone by social marketing and YouTube and tweets. Skills that people had been polishing since the Korean War were suddenly little help. Mad men sobbed into their martinis.

That's the nature of change. While you're busy plotting about how big an office you'll get with your next promotion, offices are replaced by cubicles. While you're applying to journalism school, newspapers are folding. While you're applying for your union card, the plant closes. While you're shooting the next blockbuster, everyone is staying home to watch Vines on their phones.

CHANGE OR BE CHANGED

If you crave certainty, here's what the future holds:

You can embrace change and you might fail.

Or you can not accept change—and certainly fail.

Change is the only constant. So prepare for it.

Learn to be flexible. Stretch every day; stretch your mind, your imagination, your assumptions, your body. Don't hang everything on anything but your own willingness to stay awake and connected. Ideas and rules that were once ironclad eventually rust.

Prepare to create new ideas, original thoughts, fresh directions. Hang out with innovative, adventurous, excited people. Gorge on the endless variety of new things happening.

And now more than ever, here, on what is still the frontier of an epic transformation of every connection on our planet, we need to be nimble and adaptable. We still need principles and values and a sense of what we are doing this all for. But we need to be very willing to change how we get there, to take roads heretofore untraveled and to not flinch at the strange things we see along the way.

Just to survive in these times, you need to resist the dimming past your monkey clings to. You need to open your mind, work hard, and focus on the big picture.

DOWN WITH THE STATUS QUO

The status quo is strong but it is doomed. Those who change it, win. Companies and individuals that create change are the ones that matter.

These days, that's truer than ever. People have more choices and get bored more easily. Companies that rely on traditional ways of doing things are shuttering. Customers demand novelty and improvement. Technology transforms old processes and markets. Industries that have lasted for centuries are unraveling in less than a decade. If your colleague comes up with new ideas and you hesitate to propose yours, guess who'll be cleaning out their cubicle soon?

The monkey fears change and risk. In this new paradigm, that fear imperils your life.

DON'T FEAR FEAR

Courage is not ignoring fear.

It's proceeding in *spite* of fear.

Fear is something we create in ourselves. It is the monkey's bread and butter. We can beat it. We have to start by deciding we will.

It's okay to be afraid of a new undertaking. But the monkey wants you to be afraid of fear. That's not necessary. Fear is just an early warning sign that you are taking a risk. That you are doing something brand new. It's okay to be afraid, but the monkey tells you that you should back away from what is making you feel fear. Instead you should be running toward it and getting to work.

Face fear by taking a deep breath and reminding yourself that you are creating it. Feel the fear in your body and localize it. Now try to think through what you are really scared of. What lies behind the fear? Can you boil it down? And can you face it and root it out once and for all?

EMBRACE YOUR INNER GUINEA PIG

I once had a client ask me, "If it's never been done before, why should I let you experiment on me?"

The fact that we were offering a new solution scared the crap out of his monkey. His back was to the cliff. But he was too afraid to fly. He'd prefer to do what his competition had already done before him rather than risk any sort of failure. Of course, the tried and true is only 100% reliable when the world stops turning and everything stays the same. My client faced new problems and new challenges, but he was afraid of developing new tools to face them.

It's uncomfortable thinking differently. You use new muscles, feel new aches and pains. But you can survive it and you must.

Risk can be mitigated. It can't be eliminated.

Change is the only certainty.

RE-*BEAT* THE MONKEY

If you are a creative professional, you've beaten the monkey before. You had to overcome the monkey just to get your career started. The monkey probably warned you and your parents:

"Don't be a designer, an art director, an illustrator, an architect, a musician, etc. It's too risky, the pay sucks, it's too competitive, etc."

You did it anyway.

But maybe now you're seeing that even though the monkey finally let you follow a creative career, it won't totally get off your back. It won't stay out of the idea-making process. It's always got a critique.

And maybe it's stopping you from pursuing your true passion—making art, speaking in your own voice, being your own client, your own boss, whatever.

The monkey giveth and it taketh away.

MONKEY CHOOSES YOUR DESTINY

The monkey does more than waste your time—it can derail your life. It can stop you in your tracks. It can keep you from your destiny or at best allow you to live only a pale imitation of it.

A burger chef instead of a designer.

A designer instead of a lead guitarist.

A guitarist instead of a burger chef.

Who knows what you are meant to be? Only you.

Or you can let the monkey decide.

MELISSA'S MONKEY TALE: "I was taking an AP art class my junior year of high school. We got our grades back and I only scored a 3. I wouldn't get college credit for the course; I'd wasted a whole year. Sitting there, my ego already bruised, a senior, who was already accepted to Pratt, came over, looked at my portfolio, and said, 'You made a three?!' with shock. My ego began to recover for about 3 milliseconds until he continued, 'They must not have had very many good candidates if they gave YOU a three.' At that point I was even further devastated. I had planned to apply to Parsons or FIT and to have a career in fashion design, so technically a 3 in a fine arts AP class was not the end of the world, but that incident opened a door of self-doubt that eventually led to me throwing away all my art supplies and majoring in business."

TITLES ARE FOR MONKEYS

The monkey doesn't just harangue you while you are trying to do something. It can make sure you never start. It can take things completely off the table by pinning you with a big, fat, indelible label.

It'll say:

You are just not a numbers person.

You can't manage people. Or money. Or time.

You're no good at public speaking. Or strategy. Or budgets.

You're just a creative. A poet. A child.

Things that you might have been told from a very young age have become law. Monkey law. A law that dictates you won't risk trying this new thing, because you know, in your bones, you can't. You may want to—but you aren't built that way.

Break that law.

Rip off that label.

Discover who you truly are.

And name yourself.

NEGATIVO

We are more affected by bad news than good.

We believe negative rumors more than positive ones.

We hold on to painful memories longer than happy ones.

The monkey figures that we should brace ourselves for bad situations and that good ones will take care of themselves. So when we allow the monkey to define our perspective on an issue, it becomes all-problem.

But there's a hefty price to pay. Often when we face what we see as a problem, a primal switch gets flipped. We feel under attack and our judgment is impaired. The danger spirals, everything seems bleak.

And misery loves company. When you ask most people their opinions about your idea, their feedback will likely be negative. Sure, a sunny few will say, "Great! Love it!" but when you seek input, people assume you want reasons not to proceed. They figure it's better to risk being proven wrong than to send you happily on your way. No one ever paid a consultant to tell them they were doing things perfectly. And besides, it's so interesting to look for flaws.

So look on the bright side and wait to label something as a "problem" or a "dead end." Instead, consider it just part of the process, a step along the way, and look beyond it to what you'll do next to achieve your larger goal. In the positive light of day, it might look less like a problem—and more like an opportunity.

HOW TO FIGHT A CRITIC

It's tempting to fight back against criticism. But where does it get you?

Take Edouard Manet, the father of Impressionism. Outraged by a critic's attack, Manet challenged him to a duel. They met in a forest, hacked ineffectually at each other with swords until they bent them, shook hands, and limped away. Neither man was badly injured and they both went back to work.

Take James Abbott McNeill Whistler, a thin-skinned genius whose memoir is called *The Gentle Art of Making Enemies*. When John Ruskin wrote an especially vicious review of one of his paintings, Whistler took him to court—and was awarded a farthing.

But in the long run, both men beat the critics with a different weapon—the brush. Manet and Whistler dusted themselves off and went back to their easels and the work they did there, not the opinions of long-dead critics, ensured their immortality.

Critics, internal and external, can raise any artist's hackles. They can provoke you into violent defense of your work and self-doubt. But few critics' opinions endure, because they are just products of the moment; influenced by current trends, by ignorance, by poor digestion. They are not eternal, objective, blanket truth.

Any condemnation of a work of art should only be responded to with more work. Forget swords and lawyers. Make your case with a brush, a pen, an app, a cure, a song, a page in a book.

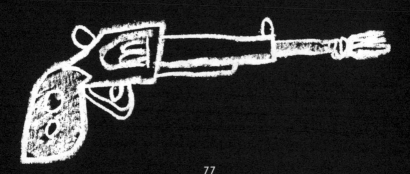

BENCH-PRESS THE MONKEY

Every artist copes with the monkey, the great ones most of all. The more productive they are, the more battle-scarred. Great artists like Picasso weren't so creative because they didn't have a monkey. It was the daily battle within that made them great.

Ali needed Frazier.

Harry Potter needed Voldemort.

Michelangelo needed the Pope.

The Yankees need the Red Sox.

The matador couldn't work without the bull.

The great learn how to suck it up and fight through. They aren't free of the monkey; they are free because of it. The monkey can help push us, fight us and, like dumbbells in a gym, makes us stronger.

THE MONKEY THINKS ABOUT YOU *ALL* DAY LONG.

BUT NO ONE ELSE DOES.

The monkey can convince you that everyone is watching and judging whatever you are doing.

That if they yawn when you speak it's because you're a bore. Not because they were up all night worrying about their meeting with you. That the reason they are critiquing your work is because it sucks and hard. Not because they feel they are being paid to say something, anything. Or because they think their boss might dislike it. Or because they're afraid of how amazingly great it is. Don't waste time dissecting their intentions. Strip their objections down to objective statements of fact. Keep only what is useful, what moves you ahead.

The fact is, you can't please 'em all. Nor should you bother to try. It's okay to live with less than 100% popularity.

Here's an experiment: Next time you have a conversation, note how often the other person's sentences begin with "I" or "me," how often they respond to whatever you say by telling you how they experience the same thing.

People are interested primarily in themselves. Whatever you do, unless it directly affects them, will be of little or no interest to them. They are not watching you or thinking about you or talking about you. Sorry. That worst case scenario the monkey worries so much about—your fly's open, you have spinach in your teeth—even if it happens, no one will notice. They're all too busy checking their own zippers.

Now that you know this, how do you feel? Seriously, if you can know in your heart of hearts that no one gives a fig about what you do, how will it change your behavior and your thinking? It'll make you bolder and braver. You'll have more confidence—because no one is really watching. You'll be truer to yourself, to the real you. You'll stand taller, speak more assertively, stand up for what you want. And instead of trying to avoid offending anyone, you'll start impressing them with your conviction instead.

Most people still won't notice you, but those who do will like what they see.

TAKES *ALL* KINDS

Here's a fact: No work of art is passionately loved by everyone forever.

Not everyone is crazy about the *Mona Lisa*, or *Sgt. Pepper's Lonely Hearts Club Band*, or *The Old Man and the Sea*. Every single work of unassailable genius still has haters. And the very thing that has won it undying fans is probably the reason others despise it.

The only work that no one bothers to take issue with is that which is utterly gutless, inoffensive and bland. It has nothing to tell us about the world. If not a soul could object, it's probably not art.

So before you struggle to please everyone, start by pleasing yourself.

REJECTING REJECTION

If you are frozen by the fear of rejection, what risks will you never allow yourself to take? What acceptance will you never experience?

If one person rejects you, do you expect all will? When your work is rejected by one person, one committee, one client . . . the monkey will help you convert that rejection into rejection of you, a rejection of all you are. And that one judge will come to represent all judges. Suddenly, one person's decision about one thing you made converts into your dismissal from the human race.

Does rejection signal the end? Or just the next step? Can you look at rejection more dispassionately, looking to understand the rejecter's methodology and motives, seeing it as an opportunity to just re-examine and maybe improve your work?

Try it. Reject the rejection.

STEVE'S MONKEY TALE: "From childhood to college I loved making art. It was fun and people praised my efforts. Then I got my first job as a junior advertising artist and I was assigned a monkey. He was relentless and rude. He informed me that no one at the agency cared about making good art, no one cared about being creative: 'Just get it done.' Any feedback he gave me was brief, blunt, harsh, or just plain rude. I was raised to respect my authority figures, but this baptism of negativity shocked me to the core. I fled—I quit. Now I know this was only my experience and that there are many amazing companies and bosses, but it's taken me almost 30 years to learn that."

RESPONDING TO
FEEDBACK

Feedback is part of creative work. People have responses to what you are making.

Clients. Employers. Customers. Reviewers. Mothers.

Some of them can insist you change what you have made. Others can just dismiss your efforts.

Don't sulk or lash out or feel rejected. Don't let the monkey stir things up. Instead, develop healthy ways to cope.

Write a detailed response in an e-mail, describing exactly how you feel, why the feedback is wrong—then delete it.

Collect a folder full of fan mail—e-mails from clients, notes from loved ones, congratulations from your boss. Then use these words of support to bolster your flagging confidence, to remind yourself that this too shall pass, and use it as counterpoint against the monkey.

Describe the grievance to a neutral friend. See how you feel about describing it. See how they respond. Once the passion of the moment cools down, maybe you'll get a fresh perspective on the most productive way to respond.

Sleep on it.

Take input as free advice, a gift, an opportunity. Skim off the emotion and look at it objectively. Imagine that you paid the critic to be a consultant to help improve your performance, that each point is pure gold that you can use to up your game. See where it takes you.

THE LIMIT'S THE SKY

It's tempting to blame limitations for limiting us. To wish we had more resources, more time, more help, more talent. But there's never enough—and you don't need it.

Limitations free your efforts and creativity, help you avoid being over-whelmed by infinite possibilities. If you have no rules, you have no game. If you have no gravity, no seasons, no wind and rain, you cannot grow. All creativity works with limits. Pushing against them moves us to new places. Limits build up pressure that pops us into new dimensions.

Hemingway used just 26 letters.

Miles had but three valves on his horn.

Painters limit themselves with canvas size, with the colors on their palettes, with the history of the artists that precede them.

Binary code limits engineers to just 111s and 000s. That limitation produced the app you just downloaded.

Shakespeare didn't use iambic pentameter just to produce plays with iambic pentameter. He used it to force himself to use new words, which expressed new ideas.

How can you limit yourself?

FRIENDS OF THE MONKEY

While your inner critic sits and plots in your head, he has allies all around. They are camped on the hill and are riding in from all points of the compass, waiting for their henchmen on the inside to lower the gates and let them flood in and maraud. Most of these confederates are unwitting. They don't even know that they are part of the plot to bring you down. But the monkey knows.

Most of these foes are driven by monkeys of their own. When you share your creative plans, your intention to take a risk or to invest in yourself, they will start chattering from the trees, gibbering in fear. Fear for themselves. When you announce your bold plans, you will set a shining example that will reflect back their own failures to live up to their dreams.

This isn't universal, of course. Many people will applaud you and offer you encouragement. But skulking in the crowd—at the back of the conference room, in a distant, dank cubicle—will be those who are resentful and bitter and frustrated. And they will begin to lob suggestions, improvements, cautions, and advocacy for the devil, designed to make you balk and backtrack.

When you are buzzing with excitement at a new project, these monkeys slink into your office, slump on to your couch and start to tell you the latest gossip, the latest management bungle, the latest reason to lose faith. They will complain about the assignment, the industry, the market. They will try to drag you into long sessions of venom and bile. They will splash you—and you've got to work to stay unblemished.

Better to get up and leave than be infected with their toxicity. They won't make it easy. They are so creative at coming up with reasons to stall and malinger, such is their monkey's gift of gab, and your own internal primate will howl with glee and strain to join the chorus. These voices get you nowhere and need not be heeded. Cut the chat short and get back to work.

If they troll around on your blog, turn off comments. If they pinch a loaf in your inbox, dump it. Delete the one-star reviews, the thumbs down

(FOM)

the snarky "friends" that aren't friends. Every opinion isn't valid. Every voice doesn't count. Listen only to the ones that will help you get to where you and your work need to be.

And, while I am busy pointing fingers, let me point them at the mirror too. For in my own moments of weakness and doubt, I have been equally capable of joining or even initiating these grumblefests, feeling insecure in myself, acquiescing to the primate within and dragging in to a colleague's office, leaning on my hairy knuckles. It's a toxic business that makes everyone feel—not purged—but depleted and sick.

MONKEY SEE, MONKEY DO

Another band of monkey pals: the media. The monkey loves the mindless vegetation of watching TV, numbing you with celebrities and gossip. Not the stories of artists and creative inspiration but the mindless doings of fabricated and often malignant chitchat. Besides being a time waster and anesthetic, the media can also skew your perception of art, artists, and the true nature of success.

Look at how the media loves the downfall of a creative person, loves to portray artists as losers and weirdos and people to avoid.

The banker is the monkey's pal too. So's the electric company, the phone company, the insurance man. They'll insist you focus just on the bottom line. Pay up! Plan for your retirement! They warn you not to take risks, to keep your day job, to be "sensible." Worry too much about money and you'll do the monkey's bidding. You'll downscale your ambitions, shelve your dreams, shackle yourself to your desk, all because you feel trapped.

Of course, the folks at the credit card company have the right to get their check. But not to decide your future.

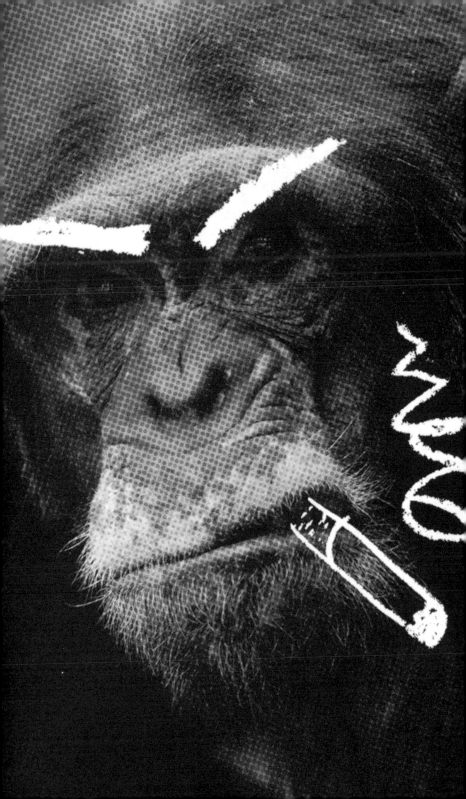

WHY WE GET PAID

Early on in my career, I went out to lunch with a family friend, a veteran copywriter, who had spent years in the trenches of the New York ad game. He took me to a restaurant just off Madison Avenue—steaks, martinis, red leather booths, autographed 8x10s on the wall—a watering hole from a bygone era.

"So, kid," he said, a Pall Mall clenched between his teeth, "How's the job going? You think advertising is for you?"

"Are you kidding?" I squeaked. "I love it. I get to think of ideas, go on shoots, work with cool people, solve problems . . . It's awesome! I can't believe I'm getting paid to do this!"

The old writer set down his highball and looked at me. "You got it wrong, son. You get to think up ideas and go on shoots. But you're paid . . . to take it."

I think that was his monkey talking to me through those clouds of cigarette smoke. The idea that being a creative professional is a perk, an indulgence, is self-devaluing nonsense. Creativity is a precious resource and those who can develop fresh solutions are invaluable, not wacky "creatives" who are lucky to be indulged. Creative people are entitled to enormous respect— from employers, clients, and from ourselves.

We don't deserve to be abused and we're not paid to take it. We're paid to make it.

MONKEY BUSINESS

If you want to make a living as a creative person, you will probably end up with some version of a client.

It could be the CMO of a major corporation.

It could be a gallerist or an art critic.

It could be the readers of your blog.

It could be the Pope.

But someone will join your creative process before it can pay the rent, and that client will have a point of view on what you are making and how you are making it. And that client, and their organization, will bring in their monkeys to add to the fun.

MONKEY, INC.

Most companies, especially big ones, work hard to maintain the status quo. After all, they spent a lot of time and money building a business model and a market and they want to protect the way things have always been done. They want to avoid risk that could upend their plans. They want to protect their management. They want to crush any competition that might try to change the game.

The people who work for these companies have big powerful monkeys of their own. That's how they keep their jobs in a big corporate structure that depends on the status quo. Risk is something to be managed and minimized. So are you.

MONKEY IN THE CORNER OFFICE

Corporate monkeys see creative people as a deal to be made with the devil. They know they need creative solutions to accomplish their goals, but they are terrified these ideas will create havoc, too. They need advertising, they need design, but they also need calendars and results and predictability. They want answers and reassurance as soon as possible. Testing, research, and other types of rational substantiation all seem like ways of making decisions that can be proven absolutely rather than made with the gut.

Simply being around creative people and part of the creative process can raise their hackles. It can be messy and unpredictable to those who need order and data and a clear, straight path. If the production process takes time or isn't clear enough, the client may want to open the oven before the cake is fully baked. And when details are not properly polished, the monkey has lots of opportunity to point out flaws. As these rough edges accumulate, the whole process begins to crumble.

Sometimes a client will see a creative solution and instantly fall in love. But then the monkey wakes them up in the night, whispering caveats and second thoughts. The done deal turns into a quagmire.

NOTHING PERSONAL

Even when you make commercial creative work, it's coming out of you. You draw from your own experiences, your own well of inspiration, your sweat, your personal taste and judgment. You throw yourself into it to make it great.

So what if they don't think it is? What are they saying about you?

When you step into a conference room and say, "Here's what I made, here's what I think is best," you are center stage. You are isolated and can feel you are wide open for judgment. If the audience doesn't get it, it can seem like they don't get you. It feels personal.

That's dangerous. If you view the questions about your work as being questions about you, the monkey will step in to protect you. It will assume that you need to avoid further risks and that will impact all the work you do thereafter. It will remind you of the pain of blazing new trails and force you to play it safe.

So when your work is judged by outsiders, by the client, by the public, you have to detach. Recognize that your work is one thing, you are another. Instead of being defensive, be open. What could seem like a hostile environment is actually an opportunity for collaboration and making the work better together.

It's not about you. And you don't need the monkey's help.

SPEAK SOFTLY AND CARRY A *BIG* BANANA

Crazy.
Unpredictable.
Irresponsible.
Unprofessional.
Childish.
Pampered.
Communist.

It's crucial to understand how you, a creative person, could appear to a client's monkey. That's how you keep the process on the rails.

If you seem like you're just following your own agenda, not listening, not aware, then your presence will be disruptive. If you are too hyperbolic in your praise of your solution, you'll be labeled a huckster. If you are low-key, you lack passion. Even if you have your own monkey on a short leash, you need to learn to manage the monkey in the conference room.

You must provide reassurance that you and your innovations take the status quo into account. That means learning to listen and to feed back key words that reassure. This isn't brown-nosing. It's getting input and giving feedback, key building blocks in the creative process.

You want to present ideas in a form that draws a direct line to the original input and shows how you are solving the problem at hand and not going off some wild "creative" tangent.

You want to empathize with the client, the company, the customer and show that you understand these problems and are here to save them.

The more you show the monkey that you are building on what exists rather than burning it down, the more the client's monkey will calm down and crawl back into its corporate cave.

PRESENTING TO THE MONKEY

Most ideas eventually need to be presented or sold to someone else. This is the monkey's last-ditch chance to nip your creativity on the launch pad—so be prepared.

First of all, literally, be prepared. Think through your presentation, step by step. Consider what needs you are addressing; the problem to be solved. Know what is expected. Understand your audience and how to talk to them. And remember: They are not your enemy, just waiting to pounce on flaws. They want you to have a great answer for them. That's why they enlisted your services in the first place.

Make sure you discuss this fully with people who are as immersed and committed to this assignment as you are. It's important to check your assumptions. But be careful when you solicit the opinions of people who may not fully understand the issues at hand. They may plant seeds of doubt that can spread. Make sure you can balance the freshness of their perspective with your deep understanding of the assignment and the client.

Your goal in this step is to build confidence with a solid foundation. To know that you fully understand what the problem is and that your solution is just that. Even if you are proposing a radical or breakthrough answer, you will know that you are grounded and secure in your recommendation.

And rehearse. In the shower, on the way to work, and finally in front of colleagues. Speaking your ideas aloud pulls them out of your head, out of the monkey's realm. You will hear the false notes and be able to correct them.

And as you present your idea, both in rehearsal and on The Day, remind yourself of why what you are doing matters. That you are solving a meaningful problem for your clients, their customers, the world. Walled out by this solid foundation of logic and preparation, the monkey doesn't stand a chance to chip away at your work.

When you are in the midst of your presentation, don't allow the monkey to suddenly pop up with some last-minute objection. He may tell you your audience is bored or disappointed or irritated. But he can't read their minds, isn't correct in his assessment of their facial expressions or their body language, doesn't know all the things they are dealing with. Don't suddenly change course because he is grabbing for the wheel, don't start making excuses or backtracking. Remain on track. Remind yourself simply that you understand the problem you were given and that you are here to help. And keep honoring your work, celebrating its freshness and insight, standing behind the ideas you have brought to the table.

When you get feedback, take it objectively. It's not about you. It's not personal. Every comment, good and bad, is another lesson, another piece of free advice that is designed to help make your work better. Some of the input will be coming from other monkeys hidden in your clients' skulls. That's why you will take your time in responding, why you'll thank them for their help in improving your idea and will incorporate all the input and return.

Don't feel you have to solve the problem right now and salvage your work on the spot. Honor your effort. It took a long time to get it as good as it is. Don't autopsy it on the conference room table. The monkey wants to make the pain of criticism go away, so he will volunteer to do triage here and now. That's not in your best interests. Accept that the verdict will actually take time to tie down, that even the critics need time to digest and process, that once you hear everyone out, you can decide how to respond.

And listen carefully, empathetically, and with an open mind. Hear what everyone has to say and just take it in. Again, don't respond or even start to mull it over. Just absorb it all. And keep your cool. Remind yourself that you came with a solution to the problem they gave you to work on. The fact that there are other factors cropping up doesn't mean you did less than great work. Take it all in. Because when you return with the revised solution, you will reference all of the things you are now hearing, showing the monkeys in the room that you heard them and have answered their concerns.

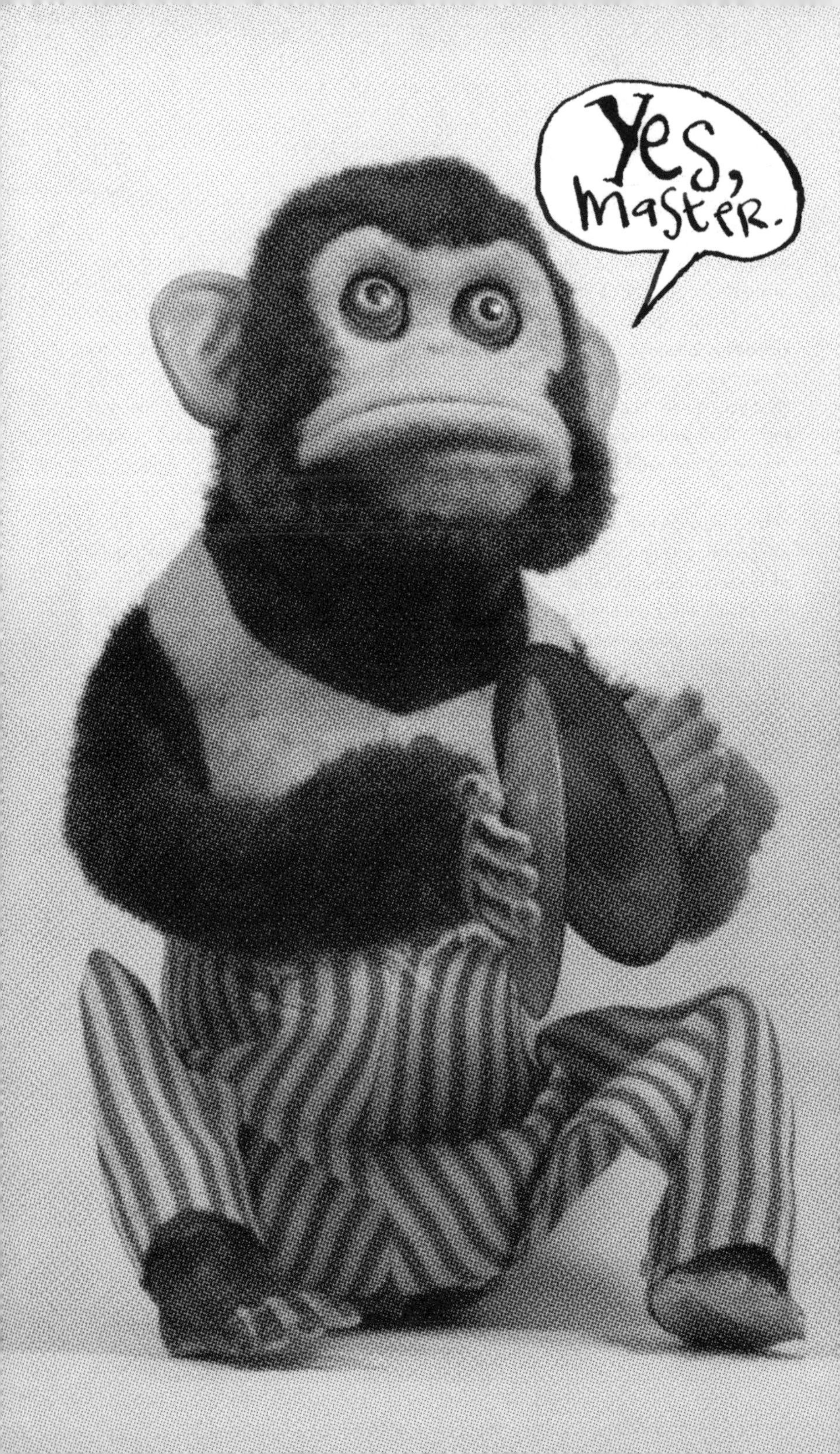
Yes, master.

Taming
the
MONKEY

KILLING THE MONKEY

Thanks for sticking with me this far, but now let's get to the reason you bought this book. Let's explore some strategies for dealing with this voice in your head.

Be forewarned, we are not going to surgically remove your monkey. He is a part of what has made you you. But he can become an increasingly unimportant part of you, like your appendix or a skateboarding scar. Like an old, corrosive friend you are slowly losing touch with.

This process of shutting your monkey is just that, a gradual closing down of habit and a reorientation of how you see the world. Don't let the monkey tell you it's all or nothing. He loves to impose rules and extremes. You can choose not to. Life is a series of waves and movements, moods and feelings come and go. If you acknowledge that, you can embrace it. Sometimes you'll feel anger or sameness, but this will pass. The same with happiness, a yen for a donut, or lust for your next-door neighbor.

Happiness isn't something to lock down and keep in a cage. It isn't a distant finish line either. But you can choose it more often than not and you can live in a way that isn't pass/fail.

The monkey is scared, rigid, and crouching in the dark.

But you are a flexible, adaptive, and happy creature living here in the now.

FIGHT!

The monkey's in one corner and you're in another. Now what? Let's begin with the most obvious strategy, one you might already have tried: Take him on. Debate him. Listen to his charges and show him he's wrong. Put him on trial.

Ask the monkey to take the stand. But this time, bring your inner lawyer to grill him, to dissect his arguments, one-by-one. You'll proceed calmly. Pay attention to the monologue. Don't engage, just observe.

Let's think of a typical situation: You're at work and you have an idea. You love it. In your gut, it feels right.

The monkey says,

> *"Your boss is gonna hate this."*

Now what?

You say, "Okay, I am imagining that my boss will hate this." That's all it is right now, right? Your imagination. Your boss hasn't actually seen it or hated it. You just have the monkey's word on that. And he's a fictional character.

So, let's pretend that your boss does hate it, then what happens?

Your monkey says,

> *"Maybe he'll fire your ass."*

Okay, let's go with it. Then what?

"He won't give you a reference and you won't be able to ever find another job."

And?

"You'll go broke and lose your home."

Okay, then what?

"You'll have to live in the street and you'll end up drinking cheap wine and huffing lighter fluid."

Huh, alright . . .

"Another bum will toss a cigarette butt and you'll catch fire and burn to death and stray dogs will pee on your ashes."

Wow, all because of this one idea you just had? Seriously? That must be one powerful idea.

Notice that the monkey's monologue is always shifting and that it is unreal. It's not what's actually going on. It's okay to hear the fantasy, but know that it is one. It's not real, just imagination.

TAKE YOURSELF TO *COFFEE*

So, how did that strategy work? It was satisfying perhaps, flushing out the absurdity of the monkey's logic, but it's not really the answer for which we're looking.

Here's the problem. Even though you may have come back at all the monkey's arguments, the effects are short-lived. You can win a street brawl, but you'll walk away dirty, scraped, your heart racing, a sour taste in your mouth. You can't do this every day. By embracing the monkey, you are tarred with cynicism, pessimism, anxiety, and negativity. It's infectious. And it won't help you do the work you need to do.

So have a look at the issues the monkey has raised and work through them on your own. It could be worth it, because buried deep within this critique is a wonderful opportunity to make better work.

Let's say you just had an experience that the monkey tells you was a horrible disaster, a failure of epic proportions that reveals how hopeless you are. Instead of being self-critical, be self-analytical. Start by avoiding value judgments; just use neutral descriptions.

Imagine your best friend asks you to have coffee with her. Then she tells you that she's been told she's worthless, inept, untalented and stupid. What would you say? Can you do the same for you?

Think about what the monkey's voice is warning you against. What is the fear? What are you really afraid of? Write it down. Describe it in detail. More detail. Keep peeling the onion. What lies behind the monkey's fear? What is the change, the risk, the newness that it is fighting? If it tells you that you won't be any good at the task at hand, what's the underlying fear?

Dig beyond the monkey's hysteria and see if you can flush out the legitimate problem.

Are there professional skills you need to hone? Are your plans currently unrealistic? Do you need more resources? More time to think through your plan?

If this is the verdict on some work you did or an action you took, write down what specifically happened. Is the problem that the situation didn't work out the way you expected? Why did you want that result? What would happen if things turn out differently? Is there anything you can take from that? Any lessons? Any opportunities? Use this assessment and this conversation with yourself as a good thing: a lesson, a creative opportunity, a way to grow.

Then turn the intensity of your feeling of fear and disappointment into fuel for the next chapter. Be grateful that soon you'll be able to do fresh work that's even better. This critique is not a reflection on you. It's an opportunity for self-analysis and self-improvement. It's a gift.

Thanks, Monkey.

SET UP A SCOREBOARD

You have accomplished a huge amount in your life—accomplishments the monkey may deny, diminish or dismiss. So once and for all, it's time to paint a more accurate picture of yourself.

Create a list of everything you have ever accomplished. All the significant things, personal and public. What you overcame in your childhood, the academic successes, the titles, the assets, all of it. Include a copy of a congratulatory e-mail from a boss, a client recommendation, a thank-you note, your report card.

If you must, juxtapose it with your failures. And then add a third column: the lessons you've learned from those failures. Did they, in fact, lead to more incredible accomplishments?

You're pretty great. Keep score.

Make sure to keep your scoreboard handy and reference it whenever you need perspective.

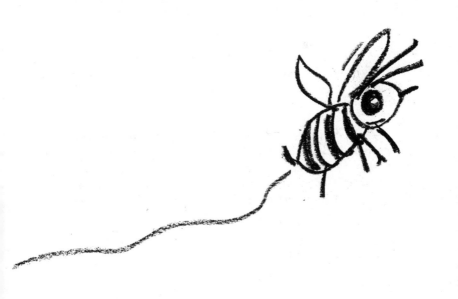

MEET THE HONEYBEE

We've tried to fight the monkey head-on by analyzing his charges. Did that work for you? If so, awesome, put this book aside for now. But I think you'll find that spending lots of time defending against the monkey's critique will have a limited, temporary effect. It'll still be you and the chimp, standing still, your fingers locked around each other's throats.

Instead we are going to try a very different strategy. The secret is so easy, so simple, it took me ages to figure it out: out-dumb the monkey and get to work.

Don't think, do.
Get the lead out. Now.

I pick up a pen and mindlessly start to draw. I don't try to figure out what I'm drawing. I don't think about whether my proportions are off, or whether the subject is interesting, or whether my butt is falling asleep, or if the ink is soaking through the paper.

I sit at my keyboard and start to write. Anything, the first words that ooze out of my fingers. Soon they start to flow and paragraphs kerchunk on the screen. I don't reread them, I don't edit them, I don't even fix my typos. I just listen to the tap dance of fingernails on plastic keys. My fingers are talking, they're singing, louder and louder, a chorus of ten—and the monkey's voice is drowned out.

Try it.

Become the buzzing honeybee, barreling out of the hive with the dawn, zooming from buttercup to daisy. Never stopping to think about whether he's doing it right, whether there's a purpose to his efforts, whether other bees are doing it better or bringing back more pollen. Just keep buzzing across the meadow, the sun on your back, your eyes on the prize, your wings churning the spring air. If the monkey speaks up, crank your buzzing louder, and keep gathering words, keep finding ideas, keep pushing that pen. Time to make the donuts. Gotta make some honey, honey.

If you insist on wondering if what you're doing's any good, just tell yourself—sure, it's awesome. Suspend judgment until later. Some of your ideas suck? So what. A lame idea beats no idea every time. Put it down, then move to the next flower.

Pick up a pen or a mouse and push it. Just make something, anything. Good, bad or indifferent. Gather the pollen. Bring it back. Let someone else worry about which diamonds are the biggest.

As you work, buzzing away, the voice will give up and fall silent. It is a bully and it can't face defeat. It's bored and can't distract you.

Bzzzzz.

BEE IN IT TO *WIN* IT

Scientists are pretty comfortable with trial and error. They know that you never know what will stick so you just gotta keep tossing ideas at the wall. The idea that seems perfect today may fall on its face tomorrow.

Failure isn't the end of the road, it's just the beginning of the next leg of the journey. So, build up the reinforcements. Back up the backup with a boatload of more ideas. Toss out a hundred lousy ideas and you'll have at least one good one.

Just don't stop at 99. The answer could be the last one to show up.

> **I haven't FAILed. I've JUST FOUND 10,000 WAys that won't WORK."**
>
> —Thomas EdiSON

THE HABIT OF WORK

Monkey thinking is a worn old groove in your brain.

When you try to start a new creative project, the voice will drive you from this new path you're on into the ditch of habitual thinking. You will slide down from the high ground into a rut heaped with low expectations and fear. You can't do this, you have no talent, you have too many responsibilities... It's a long but predictable list.

You need to develop a similarly powerful pattern of your own. The habit of regular work. Not focused on results or rewards, but just on productivity. Day after day. Immune to failure, rejection, fear. Show up and pick up your tools.

The monkey's job is to fight change, so create a new reality, a permanent state of change.

Make a rigid regimen. Live by your own rituals. Be relentless with your own discipline. Roll with the forward momentum of creative habit.

Sit down to work at the same time, rain or shine.

Always carry your tools.

Set up a nice little workspace.

Shove aside all obstacles.

Set your alarm clock. The monkey is lazy. Get up before him.

Then buzz from morning till night. One dance, one mission; no time to stop and chat.

A DAY IN THE HIVE

Here's how the bee does her job.

She gets up, she washes her face, she stretches her wings and she gets to it. She is surrounded by thousands of sisters who all have the same job description: Get out there and bring back pollen. Some of them go to the same flowers they visited yesterday, looking to bring home every drop of nectar the flower produced. Others head to a new pasture, looking for fresh flowers blooming for the first time. They don't spend a lot of time discussing the whys and wherefores. Their lives are pretty short; they have to make the most of them.

The bees are gatherers, but they are creators too. As they fly from one flower to another, they spread the flowers' DNA. They cross-pollinate, making the flowers stronger, richer, more resistant to attack. Without their hard work and energy, new life would never be born.

As the bee does her work, she doesn't pause to evaluate how she's doing. She doesn't compare the quality of her harvest to the other bees'. She doesn't wonder why she's not a queen or a cricket or a fly. She doesn't wonder if she is especially talented or lucky or likely to succeed. She doesn't check her Facebook, doesn't wonder if she looks fat, doesn't gossip about the drones.

The bee just does her work, every day, bringing back pollen to the hive, stacking it high and leaving it to the others to turn it into honey. If she thinks about her work at all, it's with pride that she is contributing, that she matters because she works.

The bee has one objective every day: To be productive. To do. To bee. Buzz, buzz.

SELF-CONFIDENCE CHOKES THE MONKEY

Self-confidence has two main ingredients: sunshine and sweat.

First, cultivate optimism however you can. Keep your eyes focused sharply on the bright side. Grin and buzz. Surround yourself with positive people: their energy is infectious. There's nothing as powerful as a group of people who all believe they can. No matter your degree of resolve, it's easy to be brought down by a Debbie Downer. Or a Harry Hater. The monkey can tell you that pessimists are the only realists, but that's hogwash. You can furnish your own reality by being positive. Not delusional—positive. Stay sunny and harness that positive energy to be productive.

Second, be a doer. Not dour. Smile and face your fears, your inadequacies, your fantasies—and act. Make things. Work. Explore. Stretch. Take risks. Go in new directions. Buzz around. It doesn't matter if you succeed every time. When you fail, you are still growing and gaining in confidence. The harder you work, the more you accomplish, the more polished your skills, the larger your confidence grows. You know what you are doing because you are busy doing it.

Bees work hard. And people call them "drones." Is that what it is? Or maybe they are just confident in their abilities. They're just busy doing what they know needs to be done: work.

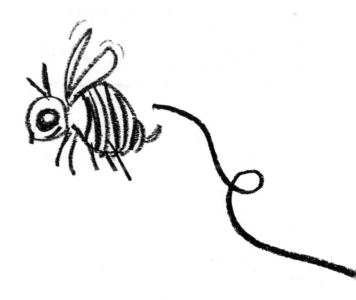

LEARN TO LOVE TO FAIL

Alright, "love" may be too strong a word. But get comfortable with it. When you accept that you are only human, you release your death grip on one of the monkey's favorite sticks to beat you with: Perfectionism. When you insist on being perfect at everything, the monkey will always show you where you came up short. It will raise your stress levels, lower your self-confidence, waste your time with picayune details, and generally make you feel like dung.

Instead, remember that mistakes aren't death sentences. They are data. They are lessons in what didn't work, designed to help improve your game. If you aren't failing, you aren't moving ahead. Love it.

THE TALENT TRAP

We imagine that a lucky few are born with a God-given gift. That they can do extraordinary things with zero effort.

But this is a dangerous myth. First of all, it convinces us that the reason we aren't successful is because we ourselves lack this gift. But the reason we fail is not because we were born unlucky. It's because we don't work hard enough and we don't have a sense of purpose. We don't fill that hive with a stream of ideas, we don't show up every day ready to roll, we don't pursue opportunities, we don't flex and bend and look for inspiration. We give in to the monkey.

And conversely, if we convince ourselves that we do have talent, why work? Why bother? It just comes naturally and effortlessly. And of course that's a dangerous trap too, because no matter where you start in the race, you won't win if you aren't willing to sweat a bit. That's why so many prodigies fizzle. That's why there are so many one-hit wonders. That's why Springsteen wrote "Glory Days."

Because "talent" doesn't guarantee success. Showing up does.

VINCENT AND THE
MONKEY

Vincent van Gogh was more than a nut who cut off his ear, never sold a painting, and shot himself in the wheat field. He was one of the most influential and productive artists who ever lived, influencing every painter who followed him for a century or more.

Amazingly, van Gogh only painted for ten years. Ten years in which he went from clumsy, muddy, pictures of grey peasants in brown fields to transcendently beautiful masterpieces like *Starry Night*, *Irises*, and the *Yellow Bedroom*.

Was he lucky? Blessed? Supernaturally talented? No, he worked his ass off. In between visits to the mental hospital, he managed to crank out more than 850 oil paintings and 1,300 watercolors, drawings, sketches, and prints. Despite a monkey that may ultimately have driven him to kill himself, van Gogh just kept his head down and knocked out a painting currently worth tens of millions—every other day.

Van Gogh summarized this entire book in a single sentence: "If you hear a voice within you say 'you cannot paint,' then by all means paint, and that voice will be silenced." Now that's genius.

OVERNIGHT SUCCESS

Some people make it look easy.

Put a video on YouTube—get a record contract.

Write a first novel—climb the bestseller list.

Date a celebrity—parlay it into a reality show.

But by the time everyone has heard of them, overnight successes have pulled a lot of all-nighters. They've played five gigs a night in small clubs in Hamburg, they've sent their manuscript to two hundred publishers, they've blogged daily for a decade, they've gone bankrupt three times.

The monkey will say you are unlucky or untalented and that's why you haven't made it. But the bee will tell you (if it stops to talk at all) that it takes a whole lot of pollen to make a teaspoon of honey. You gotta fly miles and miles every day, rain or shine, never calling in sick. You don't look back or side-to-side. You look ahead and keep on buzzing. There aren't shortcuts to success, or gimmicks or sugar daddies. You just gotta keep producing ideas—good, bad or indifferent—until you get it done.

SWEATY GENIUS

When you start any brand-new undertaking, you are more likely to fail. You don't know the rules, don't know the tools, haven't failed nearly often enough to learn the lessons. That's why most amateurs give up so early on. They never make it to their second piano lesson, their third drawing lesson, their fourth level of the video game—because they can't stomach the learning curve. The monkey tells them that their first attempt is a sign that they will never be any good, doomed on the launch pad. Lies, all lies.

One powerful monkey tool is to compare your amateur fumbling to the work of committed, professional creative people. It will tell you that you can't play the violin like Itzhak Perlman or cook like Mario Batali or write like Stephen King—because they are natural-born geniuses.

It will fail to point out that professional creatives are as good as they are because they are professional. They have committed themselves to their work. They have practiced and trained for years. They have failed and failed and brushed themselves off and kept on buzzing. The monkey makes a big deal about things like "talent" and "inspiration." But what really counts is slogging mile after mile, head down, wings humming. Sweat and perseverance are what drives "genius" to success. It's not a lottery ticket.

Don't keep comparing yourself to the greats. Instead, be inspired by their example and work ethic. Compare yourself to the bees, and keep on buzzing.

THE F✳CKET LIST

What are you afraid of? What would you never do?

Time to do it. Make a list of the things that other people seem to be able to do but that freak you out. Your discomfort list.

I'm not talking about skydiving or bungee jumping off the Golden Gate Bridge. How about:

- ☐ Singing in public?

- ☐ Eating tripe?

- ☐ Getting a physical?

- ☐ Asking for a raise?

- ☐ Wearing a bow tie?

For me, it was quitting my job, moving across the country, and finally, going to Clown School. I discovered that such an institution existed and, before I could change my mind, I paid and signed up. Two weeks later, I sat in a room with total strangers and learned how to act like a fool. I brayed like a donkey. I improvised a song about my sex life. I stared into a stranger's eyes for five minutes. I blubbered. I wore a red nose.

For three days, I made my monkey wet his pants. When it was done, I felt freer than I ever had. It made me bolder, tougher, and happier with myself than I'd ever been. Clown School is an experience I go back to whenever I face an audience or a tough decision or bad news. I saw what I am capable of.

Action emboldens.

Put your list together. Then start checking it off.

Leave your monkey speechless.

THE BEE CAN WORK MANY MEADOWS

Today I worked on writing this book. I wrote a blog post. I researched a new project. I cooked chicken thighs with kumquat relish. I did laundry. I took my dogs to the park. I drew a portrait of my neighbor. I listened to a Miles Davis album. I discussed a partnership with a friend in Europe. I read a book about Napoleon Bonaparte. And an article about Liberian graffiti.

When I suggest you focus on work to hush the monkey, you don't just need to work on the big project at hand, the one that may be hitting the wall.

Instead, turn your attention to something else that can keep you feeling creative and productive. Refill your well with something fresh you can move ahead and be successful at. What matters is momentum—keeping your wheels turning so that your energy doesn't get diverted back into the monkey's game.

And don't worry. While you are busy on this side project, the main event is still processing in your head, and soon fresh motivation will pop back to the surface.

PABLO WITH A *B*

How many Picasso paintings can you name? *Guernica? The Old Guitarist?* That weird one with the bottle and the newspaper? What if I told you Picasso made 50,000 works of art, including tapestries, plays, ceramics, poems, sculptures, and thousands of paintings. That he did 700 sketches and versions of *Les Demoiselles d'Avignon* before it was done. Was every single one of the 50,000 a masterpiece? Picasso didn't ask and didn't care.

Did he work to become successful, famous, rich? Far from it. He kept painting long after he was the most famous artist on the planet, after his works sold for over $100 million, after he was well into his nineties. Why did Picasso keep going? Because he could. Buzz, buzz.

BUILD YOURSELF A *BETTER* BRAIN

Neuroscientists have established that when you work hard on something, the composition and structure of your brain changes. You lay down neurons and weave a denser cobweb of cerebral connections. You create new brain cells that are programmed to make you better at the new things you are doing. The more brain cells you build, the more paper you dirty, the more pixels you move around, the more you move ahead.

The trick is not to focus on the end game. Not to wish mightily for the Oscar, the applause, the paycheck. Focus instead on building your skills one microscopic brain cell at a time. And you do that by putting your head (and its brain) down and getting to work.

As you work on building your mountain of ideas, you are rewiring your brain. All those challenges and fresh thinking are stimulating and feeding your neurotransmitters, creating more and more connections between your neurons, blazing new pathways, turning on dormant genes. The more you think, the better you get at it.

It doesn't matter if those ideas are good any more than it matters if you are chopping firewood or hefting kettlebells. All that counts is that you keep working, keep pumping out more ideas. Even lame creativity creates the creative mind.

BEES FLY IN ALL WEATHER

Work hard now. Don't waste time praying for inspiration.

If you're standing around waiting for a thunderbolt to strike, that's just the monkey doing weather forecasting.

And if you are tearing yourself up because you have something allegedly called "a writer's block" or "a creative block" or "a unicorn standing on your laptop," take a deep breath and go to a museum or a bookstore or the movies. "Blocks" are just the lulls between bursts of inspiration. Getting upset because pure genius isn't constantly pouring our of your fingers is a sign of nothing but impatience and misunderstanding of the process. It will come; just keep working, feeding the well, and remain calm.

These pauses are part of the process. If you make a huge deal out of them, if you label them and use them as an excuse, they will last longer. If you accept that—like any athlete or performer or genius—you need downtime and diversion, then they will be briefer and a lot more fun. Stretch your wings and get buzzing.

RUN AWAY FROM YOUR PROBLEM

Then run back.

If you feel the call of the monkey is too loud, take a break. Preferably something physical. Go for a run, hit the gym, take a walk. Or just get up stretch and take a few deep breaths. Smell the flowers, feel the sunshine. Get out of your head and get some distance.

The monkey voice builds up stress in your body, stress that feeds on itself, clouding your judgment and reason, making things seem worse than they are. When the monkey shrieks, give yourself a break.

NELLIE'S MONKEY TALE: "I wanted so very much to be an artist and just couldn't pull myself out of depression to really make any kind of serious attempt. The monkey on my back wouldn't let me. I would stay in bed, I would sleep late and often. Finally, I decided to confront the critic in my studio. I imagined what he looked like and could see him clearly. He was dressed like a cat burglar, all black and a mask, and he was carrying a pillowcase to steal from me! I talked to him and he told me I just needed to make more work. 'Make so much work that I can steal from you the ones you don't like anyway . . . just make enough that I can take what you would toss away.'

He became an ally instead of an enemy. Since that time I earned an MFA in visual culture, won loads of awards for my paintings, and even had a solo museum show."

IT *TAKES* A HIVE

Most great revolutionaries are backed by a rebel army. If you want to go somewhere scary and new, see who you can enlist to join you.

The monkey can be a lot less powerful when you collaborate with somebody else creatively.

Consider working on some projects with another person. A positive person. A person with a slightly or radically different point of view or skills.

When you collaborate, your courage increases too. You are more willing to take risks, to go boldly ahead, to focus on your goal rather than being debilitated by the status quo.

Rodgers & Hammerstein, Jagger & Richards, Wilbur & Orville. Think about how many great creative partnerships have produced amazing work. Maybe that is your destiny too.

BIG PROBLEMS ARE JUST A *HEAP* OF LITTLE PROBLEMS

You sit down to work and the monkey mutters, "How are you gonna write a book? Record an album? Start a business? It's too big. You can't do it."

How do you eat a whale? With a knife and fork, one bite at a time.

I wrote this book in sentences and paragraphs. Most of these pages started as brief notes on my phone. Ideas. Fragments. The beginnings of a mountain. Over several years, the scraps added up to what you are holding in your hand. That's how I've written my last ten books. I now have a shelf of books with my name on the spine, but I wrote them all in tiny bites.

So don't write a book. Write a word. Then another. Write it like you read. In between buses, elevators, breakfast meetings.

And if you want to develop a new skill, don't be daunted by the long journey ahead. Just walk to the corner. Then turn and walk the next block. A thousand miles, ten thousand hours, one step at time.

Soon, working on your project will become a habit. And you'll have built that mountain, a teaspoon at a time.

HOW TO WORK: THE FLIGHT OF THE BUMBLEBEE

If you must be rigid about anything, make it your schedule. Insist on sitting down at certain times and places. But let the work itself be free.

• **IT'S OKAY TO EXPLORE.** A schedule can help keep the monkey at bay—but know its limits. Don't expect to know exactly what you'll accomplish. A different outcome isn't failure. Detailed outlines and lots of tight sketches may not get you there. Have a map—but allow yourself detours. Have a destination, but let your ideas breathe and run. It's okay to take wrong paths. Don't let the monkey turn uncertainty into doubt. Live with ambiguity and just trust.

• **BE LAVISH IN YOUR PRODUCTIVITY.** Buy reams of paper and cases of pencils. Take lots of pictures. Have lots of ideas, of all qualities. Number the lines on your page and then fill them. 10 ideas before breakfast. 20 ideas after dinner.

• **DON'T QUIT MID-ROUND.** Schedule your breaks. Then even if you're feeling dry, work until the bell rings, then step away. Go for a walk or run or read or draw. You'll come back buzzing.

• **BITE BY BITE.** Remember to carve your work into digestible chunks. Don't sit down to write a novel. Write a page, sentence, a word. Then the next. One tiny bee step after another. Head down, wings moving so fast you can't see them.

• **PARK AT THE TOP OF THE HILL.** Don't stop because you are out of ideas. Push until something good comes. Stop in the middle of a sentence so you can pick it up again the next day in mid-thought. You will go to sleep excited, wake up with new connections.

• **COMMIT TO YOURSELF.** Habits don't mean habitual ways of thinking or even of working. But they are a pledge to yourself and your ultimate goal and purpose. "I'll sit down and stare at the screen and rest my fingers on the keyboard. If I do nothing else, I'll do that. I'll show up." And because you are here and dressed and appear at least to be willing, your fingers will start to move and something will start to flow from them. It may be bad, but it will be something and you will not know it is bad because you are not judging yet, right?

• **BOOK IT, DANNO.** I use my calendar to reinforce my habit. I fill my week with squares of time and name those times. I will do this then and that then. Research this on Tuesday from 2 to 4. Sketch from 8 till 10. Go to MOMA on Thursday afternoon. And when that time arrives, I am booked and I am working. Occasionally the monkey may force me to skip a square on my calendar or shove the square to the next day, but I don't delete them ever. And all those squares add up. I fill them by sitting and moving my fingers. And square by square, books emerge.

• **SPOONFULS OF HONEY.** I spend months filling files with different numbers of keystrokes and then I save them to a server in the cloud. If the monkey tells me I am wasting my time, I just look at the number of files on the server and remind myself that they are all filled with something to do with my goal. I assume they are of varying quality—some great, most useless—but it doesn't matter for now. I just fill one here, one there, and I send them to the hive.

• **HARVEST AFTER YOU SOW.** One sunny morning, I will decide it's time to look at the mountain. I will slowly work my way up and across it, reading all those words. Some will be crap. Some will be so surprisingly fresh I won't believe I wrote them. Then I will see the links between all these pieces and I will start to make piles, arranging the thoughts into larger thoughts. The things that seemed like mud will turn out to be mortar. I will notice holes and will fill them with carefully shaped new pieces. It will be easier to write these bridges because they have their parameters defined. What started as air and clouds becomes solid and logical. New ideas will protrude, ideas I hadn't intended, and I will polish them.

This is not scary because my hive is filled with lovely pollen. And it's not an aimless journey because I am filled with confidence. I know what I am doing. I built this mountain. I am too far into it for the monkey to stop me. I am not heeding him and he knows it. It's not up to me to decide if it is good. "Good" has no real meaning or value. Maybe it'll be good for you, maybe not. All that I can do is to put the pieces together and smooth the whole, moving it toward my goal, my purpose.

"I'M NOT D...

t's impossible to judge an idea when it first pops out.

So many times I've had "brilliant" ideas in the middle of the night that looked dull and familiar in the light of day. Others plop out and hit the floor like a dead fish, but days, weeks, even years later, they show how amazing and fresh they truly are. Like a fine wine or a newborn lion cub, they need breathing time to show their real nature.

That's why, even though the monkey says to judge, diminish, and condemn new ideas just need to be added to the mountain and left alone for now.

The cake's still in the oven. The idea is still incubating, growing, maturing evolving. All you can judge is its current state. And that state may well be pretty lame. You're pawing through the photos of the supermodel when she was still gangly and had braces and pigtails. Give her time. Leave your gavel on the bench.

You may come in the next day and see that the dry old stick you left on the drawing board has blossomed overnight. Hey, that's pretty good. Or the lame idea might run into another lame idea and together have a fresh new baby idea that's just gorgeous. So don't throw any pieces away yet. You may still find how they snap together.

Sometimes an idea is just a caterpillar—watch it, feed it mulberry leaves and soon it will pop out of the cocoon and blow you away.

Or maybe you'll realize that what you were trying to solve wasn't the right problem at all and that your lame idea is actually the solution to something way more important.

So bide your time, keep the oven door closed and the monkey out of the

HONOR YOUR WORK

Treat it with respect and it will be worthy.

Don't make excuses.

Don't make apologies.

Do your best and stand behind it.

When you discuss or present it, don't let the monkey hem and haw, anticipating wild objections that haven't been raised.

Respect your process too.

Give yourself the right tools to work with. Don't skimp on good materials because you worry your efforts don't merit them. Don't worry about wasting paper. Paper is cheap. Good ideas can be priceless.

Give yourself a good place to work in. Give yourself privacy. Time.

Give yourself care and respect as an artist and creator.

Don't allow anyone, most of all you, to dis what you do.

MEET THE KING

There's another creature inside you besides the monkey.

There's you,

there's the monkey,

and there's the part that hunts down ideas.

Have you ever had the experience of having an idea just pop into your head out of nowhere? Sure you have. You wake up and there's the solution. It just magically appeared.

That's the other voice. The one that doesn't waste time destroying, the one that shows you the way ahead.

It's the creative force inside you, the artist you were born to be.

It's inspiration, the Maker. It has a deep, confident purring voice.

What shall we call that?

The lion. Majestic. Noble. Mysterious. All powerful. Like Aslan in Narnia. Honor it. Go with it. Ride it to new and wonderful places.

If you work hard, the lion will appear. And when it does, you can hop onto its back and ride away, leaving the monkey far behind. You can ride out into the world and share your idea, making it a brighter place. That's the purpose of what you do, what we all do—to be inspired to solve the world's problems. It's an important job.

WHAT IT *TAKES*

The lion behaves very differently from the monkey.

It doesn't nag at you all day long. Doesn't care what you do from minute to minute, what the assignment is, what the client wants. Doesn't care what you did as kid, whether your middle school math teacher was a jerk, or if you wished you'd been a drummer. The lion is indifferent to you—until you do something to attract its attention.

If the lion does show up, you can't tell it what to do. It's not here to do your work for you. It's here to make the work you do amazing.

You can't make the lion show up. In fact, the harder you wish for it to come, the longer it will take to show up, if at all. All you can do is wait and buzz. The lion won't come over and ask you to put down the remote and join it. It waits for you to get serious. It waits to see that giant pile of work that the honeybee has been gathering.

When the lion sees you thinking and working and trying, it will come. And at its schedule, not yours. Proving your commitment may take a while. And a lot of lame ideas—but there's just no other way. You need to keep your head down and move your pen or your mouse.

Scratch, scratch, buzz, buzz, click, click—those sounds are like purring to the lion.

FEED THE *BEAST*

Another thing—you need to feed the lion. It gets thin and weak without a steady diet of inspiration, without fresh water and open plains. Your job is to feed it. You need to read books, visit galleries, meet artists, watch movies, sing songs, start hobbies, have adventures, take walks, give yourself down time. And you need to keep buzzing and avoid all monkey thoughts.

The lion needs to wander through those high piles of ideas and deep sources of inspiration: associations, blind alleys, dead ends, quotations, references, laughs, tears, and sweat. It has to roam to find prey, to cross boundaries, and you need to trust it and hang on.

YAWN!

Lions like to nap. They're awake just four hours a day. But they accomplish so much in that time. Four hours of creative inspiration will feed you round the clock.

And remember, even when the lion is slumbering, it's still the lion, still powerful, still cogitating, still killing it in its dreams.

The lion is digesting all the food you brought it, crunching the bones, licking its chops—that takes time. It eats a lot of meat.

Oh, and remember the lion is a cat; it doesn't like rain.

Keep things sunny. Optimistic. No whining. That's part of your job.

AVOID PEANUTS AND BANANAS

We feed the monkey too. We feed it with broken dreams, with fear of the unknown, with roads not taken, with the taunts of high school classmates, with our parents' failures, with envy, sloth, and greed.

But the food the monkey loves the most is a dish it wants to share with us—fear of the lion. Fear that if we do what we dream of, creating new and wonderful things, chaos will ensue, we will step into the void and surely die. The monkey is most afraid that we'll be able to break free and leave the safety of the cave forever, independent and self-sufficient, free of our past, our neuroses, our nightmares and myths. That we might actually be able to become the thing we want to be—and ride away.

Leaving home—so safe and so small.

The monkey will stand by the mailbox and block the slot. He'll scramble the number of the gallery. He'll unwrap hard candy during the recital. The monkey will point out the bad reviews, demand too much in the contract, insist on his name above the title. He is relentless, that crazy bastard. But you no longer pay him any mind.

WHERE

Will You

Ride?

THE REAL ANSWER

So far we have talked about what the monkey is, what it wants, and all the many ways it can limit your life. We have seen the power of focusing on being as productive as the honeybee and building up a big mountain of work before starting to evaluate the ideas. And we have learned about the mysterious power of the lion that can inject inspiration and magic into your creative process, if you just keep working.

But now I want to tell you about the ultimate answer to the monkey problem. And it means talking about a much bigger issue—namely, why you are here and what you can do with your life and your talents. As we discuss that, you'll see that when you shift your perspective to a much broader one, many of the niggling problems the monkey has caused you will become just faint and distant memories.

SETTING YOUR COMPASS

The lion can only take you far from the monkey if you know where you want to go.

Where will you ride the lion to?

What's your goal?

The purpose behind everything you do?

What makes you happy?

Refocus on that. Write it down. Why you are here, why you do work, what your vision is, and how it will make the world a better place. If you can sense that purpose and identify it, then you can focus on doing things that are in line with those values and goals.

Fix it in your sights: a giant sign on the horizon. And know you're going to ride the lion and get there. Focus on your bigger goal and ambition, and contributions beyond yourself.

If you have a larger sense of purpose, then you have an objective way to assess risk. To determine the correct path in any given situation. To decide whether something is dangerous—or simply new. We don't need to live in black-and-white terms, and impulsively slam on the brakes at every crossroads. Instead we can guide ourselves and we can move ahead, even through unfamiliar terrain. We know that we have to pass through this situation to achieve our goal. Risk becomes acceptable, even welcome. And that leads us forward.

ALL YOU NEED

The monkey will tell you, when it comes to something you love, like art and creativity, that making is taking, that it is a selfish act that steals time from your family and your responsibilities, and wastes time that should be spent at the office or vacuuming under the bed.

The monkey won't tell you the truth:

Creating is sharing, giving to the world, giving of yourself, your wisdom, your energy, your love and care—and when you put it out there, it returns many times.

It's a gift. That's why we creative people are called "gifted."

The world is full of new challenges and opportunities. We are surrounded by upheavals in our politics, our climate, our technologies, our connections. To build a brighter future in this heaving tangle of transformation, we need to be creative and generous and collaborative. We need to want to make a difference. We need to feel a mission in our work, because each of us makes a difference for all of us. We need to embrace a sense of purpose and obligation—not to what our moms told us when we were four or what the monkey tells us in the dark of the night or even what our banker and clients tell us we have to do to stay in their good graces. We need to recognize our purpose and know why we are here: to serve a bigger purpose, to heed a more important voice than the one that mutters in the dark.

Celebrate your creative power. See how it can change the world. See how much more important it is than the fear the monkey tries to heap on you.

Be generous. Be confident. Be brave.

THE HELP LIST

Make a list of why what you want to do matters to the world.

Who it helps.

What changes it will cause.

Use that list as a reason for doing the hard work.

Life's greatest rewards aren't money, mansions, boats and Botox. It's sharing the resources and experience we've gained with others. That's what makes us immortal. Dinosaurs still live on—in the tanks of our cars. Only by giving of yourself can you secure your place in the firmament. Even Scrooge learned that.

Who does your work help?

LORI'S MONKEY TALE: Lori was an illustrator. She made a living, but she never felt her work was truly hers. Her monkey critiqued her style, her technique, her business sense. The monkey told her to read her clients' minds and just do exactly what they asked. One day an agent told her, "If you don't respect your work, no one else will." Then Lori found a mission. Her daughter had a skin condition called vitiligo. At age 4, she started getting questions about why she had two colors of skin, why she was different. Lori couldn't find a book that would explain. So she decided to write one. At first, just like always, the monkey questioned Lori at every step of the process, trashing her drawing, her validity, her ability to deliver. Then she remembered her daughter and the importance of her project. She told me, "I figured this book was bigger than my hubris. It wasn't about me, it just needed to get done." With that, she got to work and refused to be distracted. The book was a huge success and Lori even went on *Oprah* with it. The book is called *Different Just Like Me*.

NO SMALL PARTS—ONLY BIG MONKEYS

Are you finding a cure for cancer?

Are you bringing peace to the Middle East?

Are you ending world hunger?

Maybe not. But what you make means the world to someone.

Well, what if it's just an assignment to redo a crummy brochure?

Same deal. Think through why it matters, who it helps and why. Why your client cares about it. How doing your best matters, no matter what the assignment. How this project will lead to another and a better one. How this brochure may help someone find just the thing they really need.

Treat every crummy project as if it really truly matters and soon you'll see that it does. It matters most of all to you because what you do is important and you should treat it so. And the more you do that, the more you value your contribution, the larger the opportunities that will come to you.

The lion can carry you far. Just lighten the load by kicking the monkey to the curb.

PAYBACK TIME

Think of all the people who've inspired you. The authors you love, the directors whose movies have moved you, the musicians who kept you company in the studio—all of them. And now think of your creative work as payback. Don't be intimidated by the people you admire; see your work as a way to pass on the favor.

Maybe your mentors will see your work and be inspired by it. I've had that experience and it is one of the most gratifying in life. Or maybe your work will inspire a stranger, someone in need of your help. That is the greatest gift you can give. The most generous thing you can do is to give anonymously, and your work has the potential to do that.

Think about these things next time the monkey is trying to squash your productivity. Think of those who won't get to benefit from your unborn work.

WHY DO YOU DO WHAT YOU DO?

Why do you do whatever creative things you do?

The paycheck? The health plan? The admiration from the neighbors?

No, you do it, whatever form it takes, because you must. Not because it's what someone told you to be or to do but what makes you feel good and right. Because it grows out of who you are and how you want to see the world. Because it's your mission.

That's right, it's not just Air Force pilots, young Mormons and CEOs who have missions. We can all have a purpose that's bigger than we are, bigger than our petty concerns and fears. When we raise that mission like a banner, we connect with others who share that dream. We feel more empowered and fulfilled and happy.

Your work matters. Figure out to whom. Figure out why. And if that seems impossible, then why are you spending your time doing it?

Life is short and getting shorter. Rock the boat. Take a risk. Do something worth carving on your headstone.

Figure out your purpose and then ride the lion toward it.

VINCENT AND THE
MONKEY

Long after he was dead and buried, Vincent van Gogh has been diagnosed with everything from schizophrenia to syphilis. He may have been bipolar or epileptic, eaten too much paint or drunk too much absinthe. Did van Gogh have a monkey too? Certainly. He had plenty of problems and one or more of them led to the events of the 27th of July, 1890, when he shot himself, in the chest, in a wheat field. He hung around for another day and a half, said, "The sadness will last forever," and died.

Van Gogh was 37 and he had been painting for just ten years. In that time he accomplished so much, producing hundreds of beautiful works of art that have influenced artists ever since. His life, short though it was, left ripples.

But what if he hadn't cut his life so short? What if he had lived to 86 like Monet? Or 84 like Matisse? Or 91 like Picasso? What paintings might now hang in museums? What directions might he have taken the art world? How might we all see differently than we do? Try to imagine all he never had the chance to imagine.

So much beautiful art has been made through the course of human history. But there is so much beautiful art that was never made, never sketched or painted or framed or hung. The monkey does the job of that pistol in Auvers-sur-Oise every day, cutting creative careers short, stifling ideas, throwing up roadblocks to new horizons. Every time the monkey forces a creative person to give up, the world is robbed of ideas that could lead to answers and inspiration and gasps of delight.

You can't know what impact your work could have on the world. Don't let the monkey decide for you.

THE WORLD NEEDS YOU

The world needs change.

The world needs fresh solutions.

The world needs great design.

The world needs to fix the mistakes of the past.

The world needs to ride the lion.

Work hard.

Be good to yourself.

Know your purpose.

And

SHUT YOUR MONKEY!

NOTES TO SELF: MY MONKEY TALE

WHAT THE MONKEY SAYS TO ME:

HOW THE MONKEY LIMITS ME:

WHERE THE MONKEY COMES FROM:

HOW I CAN FIGHT BACK:

WAYS I CAN FEED THE LION:

WHERE I WANT TO RIDE:

MORE BOOKS
MONKEYS HATE

If you need additional ways of keeping yourself inspired and buzzing like a honeybee, consider some of the books that help me to keep motivated.

- **BIG MAGIC** — Elizabeth Gilbert
- **LUST FOR LIFE** — Irving Stone
- **REWORK** — Jason Fried and David Heinemeier Hansson
- **START** — Jon Acuff
- **THE CREATIVE HABIT** — Twyla Tharp
- **THE CREATIVE LICENSE** — me
- **THE ICARUS DECEPTION** — Seth Godin
- **THE POWER OF NOW** — Eckhart Tolle
- **THE WAR OF ART** — Steven Pressfield
- **WHAT IS ART AND 100 OTHER VERY IMPORTANT QUESTIONS** — Ernst Billgren

ABOUT THE AUTHOR

Danny Gregory has spent three decades as one of New York's leading advertising creative directors and has created award-winning global campaigns for clients like Chase, JP Morgan, American Express, IBM, Burger King, Ford, Chevron, and many others.

Danny has written many internationally bestselling books on art and creativity. He is also cofounder of Sketchbook Skool, an online creativity school that has inspired tens of thousands of students around the world. He is a frequent speaker on creativity at schools and corporations around the world.

For more, visit dannygregory.com.